Slow Cooking for Two

Slow Cooking for Two

A SLOW COOKER COOKBOOK WITH 101 SLOW
COOKER RECIPES DESIGNED FOR TWO PEOPLE

MENDOCINO
PRESS

Contents

Introduction

Most people associate slow cookers with their mother's pot roast or big batches of game-day chili, but when you're cooking for two, these handy appliances are your best friends, enabling you to whip up great meals with little mess and even less waste.

With schedules becoming ever more hectic, everyone is looking for ways to save time in the kitchen, but we still want to eat food that is healthful and tastes good. Having a slow cooker or two allows you to prepare meals hours in advance, leave the house while your food cooks, and return to a fuss-free dinner that is ready to eat.

In this book, you will learn how to prepare delicious and nutritious meals in a small slow cooker that will feed just the two of you. While more than 80 percent of American households own a slow cooker, most recipes are developed for the larger appliances, serving four to six people. Unfortunately, you can't just put less food into a slow cooker for a smaller yield; you have to use a smaller appliance. All of the recipes in this book were developed for the 1-½ to 2-quart slow cookers. You can use either one for all of these recipes.

You will learn a little about the mechanics of the slow cooker as well as the benefits of this cooking technique and tips for success. You'll also learn what to stock in your pantry, how to shop for two, and easy and fun ways to prepare and store food safely.

A slow cooker not only saves time; it also saves money and can improve your health. With little preparation and long cooking times, you don't have to spend much time in the kitchen to produce excellent meals with this appliance. Cooking at home rather than eating out or buying prepackaged processed food is less expensive and helps you avoid additives such as salt, sugar, fat, colorings, and other chemicals that may adversely affect your health. And the food that comes out of the slow cooker is delicious—well seasoned, tender, and perfectly cooked.

While slow cooking is easy, cooking for two does present some challenges. Recipes that produce just enough food for two people are fairly rare, and not all higher-yield recipes work well when the ingredients are simply halved. Certain ingredients are also packaged in larger quantities than what you'll need for two servings. While cooking for two, you'll have to take some time to wrap and freeze ground beef and chicken from larger packages, or safely store canned and jarred ingredients if all are not used in a recipe. You'll also have to learn how to shop differently, choosing smaller quantities and seeking out smaller prepackaged food items.

But there are advantages to cooking in small quantities, too. When you're cooking for two, you can splurge occasionally on special ingredients that would simply be prohibitive to buy in large quantities, such as exotic mushrooms, lobster, asparagus, saffron, or fresh berries that are out of season.

This book will help you use simple cooking techniques to get the most out of your smaller slow cooker. You'll learn how to cook an entire meal in the slow cooker using cooking bags, and get tips for getting the most out of meats and vegetables with some judicious precooking. And when a recipe serves more than two, you'll find tips and easy recipes to turn leftovers into another feast.

PART ONE

Getting Started with Slow Cooking

CHAPTER ONE

The Basics of Slow Cooking

The slow cooker is very easy to use, but there are some rules you need to follow for best results. First, it's important to understand how this jack-of-all-trades appliance operates. The slow cooker consists of a heating element that completely surrounds a crockery or stoneware insert. The insert is either removable or attached to the heating element. The insert heats up and maintains a constant heat so the food cooks slowly and gently. The lid on the slow cooker keeps steam inside the appliance, trapping flavors and nutrients. It also forms a seal with the insert, so the temperature inside the appliance stays constant.

The slow cooker heats up rapidly to bring the food quickly above the danger zone—from 40°F to 140°F—where bacteria can grow and thrive. Then the temperature stays constant to finish cooking the food. Recipes usually have a cooking time of six to eight hours. That long time period lets flavors develop and makes meat and vegetables extra tender.

You can cook some surprising foods in the slow cooker. Recipes such as casseroles, soups, and stews, of course, are a natural for this appliance. But did you know you can also make cheesecake, main-dish salads, risotto, sandwich fillings, and roasted vegetables in the slow cooker? This appliance can be more versatile than you ever dreamed.

WHAT IS SLOW COOKING?

Slow cooking is, well, cooking food slowly! Braising in the oven, smoking on the grill, and simmering on the stove top are all slow-cooking methods. But for this book, slow cooking means cooking food in a special appliance called a slow cooker.

Owning a slow cooker (or two or three) is like having a personal chef at your disposal. This wonderful appliance leaves you free to accomplish other chores while dinner is cooking. It does all the work for you! All you do is add ingredients, turn it on, and go about your business as it cooks the food to perfection.

Slow cookers come in many sizes, from a small 2-cup version used to make dips or appetizers to monster 7-quart appliances that can cook a large roast or ham. When you're cooking for two, the best sizes to use range from 1 to 2 quarts. With the smaller models, you'll have just enough food for the two of you. The larger size will let you dish out two generous servings with perhaps some left over for another meal or another recipe.

The slow cooker reaches temperatures of about 200°F on low and about 300°F on high. This cooks food safely and thoroughly. The low heat and moist cooking environment turn inexpensive cuts of meat into moist and juicy bites that melt in your mouth, and cook hard root vegetables to perfect tenderness. Because the slow cooker is a closed environment, no flavor compounds are lost in steam, so the taste of food deepens and becomes more complex.

Recipes from any cuisine around the world can be made in the slow cooker. You can enjoy Italian lasagna, Indian curry, Mexican enchiladas, and classic American pot roast with this wonderful appliance.

BENEFITS OF SLOW COOKING

There are many benefits of slow cooking. Most of the time, you don't need to stir, turn foods, or watch the food as it's cooking. Your time savings can be significant. While some foods should be cooked before being added to the slow cooker, many foods can go directly into the stoneware insert without sautéing.

Slow cooking saves money, too. Inexpensive cuts of beef, such as chuck roasts and brisket, as well as pork roasts and chicken thighs, cook better in the slow cooker than more expensive steaks, tenderloin, and chicken breasts do. The moist, low-heat environment breaks down connective tissue in the tougher meats and makes them very tender.

The slow cooker uses very little energy compared to other appliances. Set on low, the smaller slow cookers use about as much energy as a 75-watt light bulb, which costs about $0.02 per hour. In comparison, using an electric range costs about $0.05 per hour, and a toaster oven costs about $0.69 per hour to operate.

. . . .

The slow cooker is a wonderful tool for beginning cooks. As long as the time and temperature instructions for each recipe are followed, food should not burn or overcook. If you are new to cooking, the slow cooker is a great place to start. And success will give you confidence so you'll be more likely to try new recipes and other cooking techniques in the future.

. . . .

Finally, slow cooking is healthful cooking. When meats and vegetables are cooked at high heat, compounds called advanced glycation end products (AGEs) are formed from protein, fats, and sugars. Those compounds are linked to an increased risk of heart disease, diabetes, and cancer. The low-heat slow cooking of the slow cooker doesn't produce AGEs. Also, since the slow cooker is a closed environment, fewer of the water-soluble vitamins, such as B complex and vitamin C, escape in steam. They remain in the flavorful liquid to nourish you. And since slow cooking generally uses steam to cook food, very little oil is required in these recipes.

NOTES ON EQUIPMENT

Before you purchase a slow cooker, do your research. Slow cookers are equipped with many different features, so you should know what you want to accomplish with this appliance before you buy one.

- Slow cookers come in round and oval shapes. The oval shape is more adaptable, since you can cook larger cuts of meat in that appliance.
- Programmable slow cookers let you choose how long you want the food to cook and at what temperature. You can even program the appliance to stop cooking and keep the food warm for a few hours. Unfortunately, it's difficult to find programmable slow cookers in the smaller sizes.
- Some slow cookers come with accessories so you can travel with them. Lid straps and insulated carriers or travel bags will help keep the food inside the appliance and keep it warm while you travel.
- If you have the option, choose a slow cooker with a removable insert for easier cleaning.

Know Your Slow Cooker's Temperature Range

A few years ago, manufacturers started increasing the cooking temperature of slow cookers. Older slow cookers cook at about 180°F on low and 240°F on high. Now they cook at 200°F on low and 300°F on high. This means that the timing for older recipes will be off. With a new slow cooker, the food may burn if you cook according to those recipes.

To solve this problem, if you have an older slow cooker, check the temperature: Fill the slow cooker two-thirds full with cool water, cover, and turn it on low. After four hours, check the temperature with an instant-read thermometer. If it is 180°F, you'll need to add some cooking time to the recipes in this book. Check the food with an instant-read thermometer according to the recipes. You may need to add about 20 percent more cooking time. And if you have a new slow cooker, reduce the cooking time if you follow older recipes.

Manufacturers are developing fun new slow cooker options. Some newer-model slow cookers now come with three different inserts. This will give you the freedom to cook food in larger amounts for parties if you'd like. There are also slow cookers that attach to each other for buffet serving. These "Hook Up" slow cookers usually come in 1- to 2-quart sizes and link onto each other through an electrical connection. They are a wonderful choice for cooking for two because you can cook an appetizer, main dish, side dish, and dessert all at the same time!

SLOW COOKING TECHNIQUES

The slow cooker uses moist heat to cook food, as compared to the dry heat of the oven and grill. Food steams, braises, and stews in the slow cooker. This turns connective tissue in tough cuts of meat into gelatin, which adds delicious feel and body to the liquid. The moist heat also softens vegetables and brings out their flavor.

Choose the correct size of slow cooker according to the volume of food you want. Slow cookers should be filled between half and three-quarters full for best results. If you fill the slow cooker less than half full, the food could overcook and burn. If you fill it more than three-quarters full, liquid produced by foods may overflow the appliance, or foods could undercook.

- While many foods can go into the slow cooker with very little preparation, some foods need to be precooked, either in the microwave oven or on the stove top. For best results, follow the directions in the recipe. Meat may be browned, or onions and garlic may be sautéed, to add more complex flavor.
- One hour of cooking on high is equivalent to two hours of cooking on low. For instance, if a recipe says to cook for eight hours on low, you can eat sooner if you cook for four hours on high.
- Some foods, such as tortes and meat loaf, should be cooked in a foil sling. To make a sling, tear off two 24-inch lengths of foil. Fold them in half lengthwise, then fold them in half lengthwise again. Place the strips in a plus-sign formation in the bottom of the slow cooker, and then add the food. Use the strips to lift out the food when it's done cooking.
- Don't add too much liquid. Foods such as meat and vegetables will release liquid as they cook. Since liquid does not evaporate in the slow cooker, the appliance may overflow or the food will be diluted and flavorless if you add more than the recipe calls for.
- You usually don't need to stir or manipulate food as it cooks. But some foods, such as risotto and pasta recipes, do call for stirring. Make sure you stir from the bottom for even cooking.
- The liquid that is extracted from the food as it cooks contains wonderful flavor. Most people enjoy that liquid thickened into a sauce or gravy. There are two easy ways to do this: You can flour the meat before you add it to the slow cooker. Or you can thicken the liquid at the end of the cooking time. To do so, dissolve about 1 tablespoon of cornstarch or flour in ¼ cup of water or the cooking liquid, then stir it into the slow cooker. Cover and cook on high for 15 to 20 minutes or until the liquid is thickened.
- The outside of the slow cooker will become quite hot as it cooks. Make sure the electrical cord doesn't touch the insert. And keep small hands away from the appliance. You may want to rest the slow cooker on a tile or sturdy trivet to keep it away from your laminate or tile countertop, since the heat generated by the slow cooker might damage that surface.

FOOD SAFETY

Food safety is a critical component in cooking. If someone gets sick because the food you prepared is contaminated with pathogenic bacteria, it doesn't matter how good it tastes or how healthful the food is. All of the cost savings you enjoyed by using the slow cooker will be spent on medical bills.

If the power goes off while the slow cooker is on, you have a few options. If you are at home, finish cooking the food in a pot on the grill or on the gas stove, if you have one. If you were away while the power was off, you must discard the food. You really have no way of knowing how long the power was off. Eating that food is too much of a risk.

The basic food safety rules of clean, separate, cook, and chill apply to the slow cooker, too. Follow these rules to the letter to make sure your food is safe as well as delicious.

- **Clean.** Wash your hands before cooking and after handling raw meat, poultry, and eggs. Rinse vegetables and fruits under cool running water before adding them to the slow cooker. Scrub sturdier produce such as potatoes, carrots, and apples with a soft brush. Wash surfaces, utensils, and plates with soap and water after they come into contact with raw meat, poultry, and eggs.
- **Separate.** Keep raw meats, poultry, and eggs away from foods that are eaten raw or are not cooked. Never transfer cooked foods to a platter that held raw meats.
- **Cook.** Always cook food to a safe internal temperature and check that temperature with a reliable instant-read thermometer. Whole cuts of beef should be cooked to 145°F, whole cuts of pork should be cooked to 145°F, whole fillets of fish should be cooked to 145°F, and whole chicken and chicken breasts should be cooked to 165°F. Ground meats should always be cooked to 165°F. You must always assume that the raw meat you buy is contaminated with bacteria. Handle with care.
- **Chill.** When you are done eating, promptly refrigerate cooked, perishable foods within two hours, or within one hour if the air temperature is above 90°F. Separate larger amounts of food into shallow containers, cover, and refrigerate. Don't be afraid to put hot foods into the refrigerator. It's made to handle them. The food will cool down quickly as long as it is properly packaged.

TEN TIPS FOR SLOW COOKER SUCCESS

Here are ten tips for success so you can enjoy delicious and healthful meals using your slow cooker for years to come. Follow these strategies for best results.

1. **Keep the lid on.** Every time you lift the lid, you need to add 20 to 30 minutes of cooking time to the recipe. If you are using a circular slow cooker, you can simply spin the lid as it sits on the insert to remove condensation so you can see inside. Your best bet, however, is to follow the recipes closely and only remove the lid after the recommended cooking time.

2. **Plan ahead.** Cooking for two means planning your meals and shopping trips a few days in advance. For instance, when you purchase a pound of ground beef, immediately divide it into smaller portions and freeze some of it. If you're going to use a cup of chicken broth in a recipe, refrigerate the rest and plan to use it in another recipe later in the week. Remember that wasting food is wasting money.

3. **Deglaze the pan when browning meats.** If you choose to brown meats before cooking them in the slow cooker, always deglaze the pan. Just pour a little water or broth into the pan, scrape up the brown bits stuck to the bottom, and add them to the slow cooker. That material, known as *fond*, is full of wonderful and rich flavor!

4. **Taste the food before you serve.** Slow cooking can mute the flavors of herbs and spices. Before you serve, taste the food. Add more salt, black pepper, herbs, or spices if you feel it is necessary.

5. **Start cooking on high.** If you or your partner are pregnant or in a high-risk health group, start every recipe by cooking the food on high for one hour, then turn it to low (remember to adjust the overall cooking time of the dish using the ratio of one hour on high equals two hours on low). This will quickly bring the food through the danger zone when bacteria grow more quickly, so the food will be safer.

6. **Know your slow cooker.** The first time you use your slow cooker, stay home and monitor the cooking process. The cooker may have hot spots, or may cook faster or slower than you think. Once you understand how your slow cooker cooks, you can leave the house while it's working.

7. **Use an instant-read thermometer.** A reliable, good-quality food thermometer is a necessity when cooking poultry, pork, and beef. Always check the temperature of these foods before you serve them, and know the safe final internal temperature of each type of meat: 145°F for fresh beef, 145°F for pork, 145°F for fish fillets, 165°F for whole chicken and chicken breasts, and 165°F for ground meats.

8. **Add acidic ingredients at the end.** Acidic ingredients such as tomatoes, vinegar, and wine can prevent beans, potatoes, and some root vegetables from softening properly as they cook. Cook these ingredients to the desired consistency, and then add acidic ingredients.

9. **Remove food promptly.** Be sure to remove your meal promptly from the slow cooker. Residual heat can keep cooking the food and it may overcook. Don't use the crockery insert to store food in the fridge because the thick walls will slow down the cooling process. And don't use the slow cooker to reheat food, because it will pass through the danger zone too many times.

10. **Experiment!** Once you're comfortable with your slow cooker, start branching out. Start with a recipe you have made before and substitute different cheeses, meats, vegetables and herbs and spices to make the recipe your own.

CHAPTER TWO

A Guide to Slow Cooking

Using your slow cooker will become second nature after you make only a few recipes. Still, there are some rules and guidelines about cooking, shopping, and preparing food for two that you should know before you begin.

Understanding portion sizes is key when you are cooking for two. Generally, one serving consists of about ¼ pound of beef, chicken, or pork, and 6 ounces of fish or seafood. For grains, about 1 cup of rice or pasta is considered a serving. Produce is different; about half of your plate should be fruits and vegetables. Most people should eat 2 to 4 cups of fruits and vegetables every day.

As you use your slow cooker, you'll discover pretty quickly how much food you eat. And the amount of a main dish you eat depends on what you serve with it. For instance, if you serve a substantial green salad and some toasted whole-grain bread with your meal, you'll probably eat less of the main dish.

If you do make too much food at first, remember that most recipes freeze very well. Portion the leftover food into freezer containers, then label, and freeze for up to three months. Or you can use the leftover food in other recipes. Roasted Vegetables (page 72), for instance, are delicious mixed with some cheese and enclosed in pizza dough, then baked at 400°F for 20 minutes for calzones. Or leftover Creamy Parmesan Risotto (page 78) can be formed into small cakes, rolled in bread crumbs, and sautéed in butter to make risotto cakes.

PANTRY FOR TWO

A well-stocked pantry is essential for any kitchen. What you choose to put in your pantry depends on what you like to cook and eat, but most pantries should include the basics used in many of these recipes.

The pantry is defined as the shelves and drawers in your kitchen, the refrigerator, and the freezer. All stored foods should be well labeled and tightly closed in secure containers. It's a good idea to keep a running list of the foods stored in these places so you know what you have on hand and when it's time to add ingredients to the shopping list.

When you're shopping, make sure that you check the label for how the food should be stored and the expiration date. Many foods are kept in the cupboard before they are opened, then must be stored in the refrigerator for food safety reasons.

Make sure that you rotate foods in the pantry, refrigerator, and freezer. Use foods that are older and closer to the expiration date rather than foods you just purchased.

Expiration dates don't always mean the food is no longer fit to eat. There is no federal standard on expiration dates for food safety. The dates stamped onto cans, bottles, and boxes mean that the food quality is maintained until that date. You don't have to throw away canned foods, pasta, rice, beans, and even condiments if they are a little past the expiration date. Do pay attention to dates on perishable foods such as bagged salads, meats, eggs, and cheeses, however. Those items may be unsafe to eat after the expiration date has passed.

These are the staple foods to keep on your kitchen shelves (read the labels to see if they need to be stored in the fridge after they're opened):

- Canned beans
- Canned broths and soups
- Canned fruits
- Canned meats and seafood
- Cereals
- Condiments such as mayonnaise, mustard, and ketchup
- Couscous
- Crackers
- Dried soup mixes
- Extra-virgin olive oil
- Flour
- Herbs and spices
- Jams and jellies
- Nuts
- Onions
- Pasta of different shapes
- Peanut butter
- Potatoes
- Salsa
- Sugars
- Syrups and honey
- Tea
- Vinegars, including apple cider, red wine, and balsamic

These are the staple foods to keep in your refrigerator:

- Butter, unsalted
- Eggs
- Milk
- Refrigerated doughs
- Salad dressings
- Salad mixes
- Sour cream
- Yogurt

These are the staple foods to keep in your freezer:

- Chicken
- Coffee
- Frozen doughs
- Frozen pasta
- Frozen precooked meatballs
- Frozen vegetables and fruits
- Homemade soups, broths, and stocks
- Ice cream
- Meatless proteins
- Meats, divided into individual portions
- Nuts

SHOPPING FOR TWO

Whether you're shopping for two or ten, making a list is the first step. Look through this book and choose some recipes. Add other foods to your menus, such as green salads, toasted rolls, or some fresh fruit. Write down the menus for the week. Then make up your shopping list. Think about what you can use that you already have on hand.

Go to the store when full; never shop when you're hungry! Stores are designed to entice you into buying everything from sticky buns in the bakery to candy bars at the checkout line. Follow your list, but keep your eyes open for sales and bargains on food you know you'll want to eat.

When you're shopping for two, look for bargains on products in smaller sizes. For instance, shelf-stable Alfredo sauce is usually sold in 16-ounce jars. But refrigerated Alfredo sauce comes in a container that holds just 10 ounces. You can find 5-ounce cans of evaporated milk as opposed to the more typical 14-ounce cans, and smaller boxes of pasta.

Meats and poultry are usually the most expensive items on your shopping list. You can ask the butcher to break up a larger package of beef short ribs, for instance, into just two or three ribs for the two of you. Never be afraid to ask for help! And if you see a great bargain on a 5-pound package of sirloin tips, for example, buy them if you have room in your freezer. Divide that package into ½-pound portions, then label and freeze them. Plan to use them within six months.

TIPS FOR PREPARING AND STORING FOOD

Most foods go into the slow cooker with little preparation, but there are still some rules to follow for best results. These tips will help you prepare and store food.

- Make sure that all of the vegetables you put into the slow cooker are cut about the same size so they will cook evenly. This is especially important for root vegetables, which generally take the longest to cook. Follow instructions for layering the food according to the recipe.
- Pay attention to how meats are prepared. Some cuts are put into the slow cooker whole; others are chopped or cubed. Sometimes the meat is cooked with the bone in, while other times the bone is removed. And sometimes meats are browned for better flavor before being cooked in the slow cooker.
- When the food has finished cooking, remove it from the slow cooker promptly. Any leftovers should be refrigerated within two hours after the food is done.
- Make sure you keep the pantry, fridge, and freezer clean. The pantry should be cleaned once a month. Remove everything, wash down the shelves, and discard and replace foods older than one year.
- Clean the fridge every two weeks by removing everything, throwing away anything that is spoiled, and washing down the shelves.

- Empty the freezer every six months. Throw away anything that has freezer burn (dehydrated areas of the food), defrost the freezer if necessary, and update your list of what the freezer holds.
- Divide any leftovers into shallow containers, then cover, label, and refrigerate or freeze them. Use refrigerated leftovers within three days. Frozen leftovers can be kept for three to six months.
- If you're going to use only part of a can or jar, you must refrigerate the remaining contents. Always remove food from a can and place it in a container with a tight seal. Label the food and store it in the refrigerator. Foods in glass jars can just be tightly closed and refrigerated; plan to use the rest within a week or two.

TECHNIQUES FOR SLOW COOKING FOR TWO

The techniques for slow cooking for two are the same as for larger slow cookers. The only thing that really changes is the amount of food you're cooking. With smaller slow cookers, food will be less likely to burn if the appliance isn't half full. Follow the recipe carefully, especially the first time you make it, and use an instant-read thermometer to check the final temperatures of meats, fish, and poultry.

Tougher and less expensive cuts of meat cook beautifully in the slow cooker. In contrast, that expensive filet mignon will become tasteless and dry if you cook it in this appliance. Inexpensive meat is an ingredient in many of the recipes in this book because it cooks so well in a moist environment.

How to Cook Meats

The best cuts of meat to use in a slow cooker include:

- Beef: blade, boneless ribs, chuck, round, rump, stewing beef
- Chicken: drumsticks, thighs
- Pork: chops, country ribs, ham, rib roast, shoulder

Meats such as beef roasts, pork, and lamb become tender and juicy when cooked in the slow cooker. All you have to do is add them to the appliance and turn it on. For best results, follow these tips:

- Ground meats should always be browned and drained before being added to the slow cooker. If you skip this step, the meat will be mushy and not develop much flavor, and there will be too much fat in the finished dish.
- To add delicious flavor, you may want to brown beef roasts in a bit of olive oil on the stove top before placing them in the slow cooker. Cook the roast for a few minutes on each side, turning it with tongs, until it is brown. Remember to deglaze the pan and add the delicious drippings to the slow cooker!
- Don't cook frozen meats in the slow cooker. The frozen meat will hold the temperature down, keeping foods in the danger zone of 40°F to 140°F for too long.

- Trim excess fat from beef and pork before cooking. The fat will raise the temperature of the liquid in the slow cooker and the dish may overcook. In addition, that excess fat will melt into the liquid, making it unpleasantly greasy.
- Game can be cooked in the slow cooker, but because these cuts have a strong, gamey taste, the whole dish will be very strongly flavored. If you choose to cook game, add extra fat to the recipe, since this meat is usually very lean.

How to Cook Poultry

Poultry and the slow cooker were made for each other. Whether you choose whole cuts of chicken or turkey, ground poultry, or chopped or sliced poultry, you will be pleased with the results.

- Dark meat chicken, such as thighs and drumsticks, will give you better results than white meat chicken because of the higher fat content. Dark meat becomes very tender and will not overcook, while chicken breasts can become dry.
- Remove the skin from poultry before cooking. The skin will never become crisp and it adds extra fat to the recipe. If you want to leave the skin on chicken breasts or thighs, brown them well on the stove top before you add them to the slow cooker. You can also remove the skin from breasts and thighs after cooking.
- Chicken wings should always be browned—either before or after cooking, according to the recipe— since it is almost impossible to remove the skin from this cut of poultry.

How to Cook Fish and Shellfish

Fish and shellfish present a challenge in slow cooking. Since this type of food is very delicate, it doesn't take long to cook. Fish soups and stews should be made by cooking all of the other ingredients, then adding the fish during the last 20 to 30 minutes of cooking time.

Shellfish such as shrimp and scallops cook in about 5 to 10 minutes. Whole salmon and fish fillets can be added during the last 20 to 30 minutes of cooking time, while cubed fish cooks in 10 to 15 minutes.

You can cook these types of seafood in the slow cooker:

- Clams
- Mussels
- Salmon steaks and fillets
- Scallops
- Shrimp
- Tuna steaks
- White fish fillets such as halibut, red snapper, and cod

How to Cook Vegetables

Carrots, potatoes, onions, garlic, parsnips, sweet potatoes, and other sturdy vegetables are perfect choices for the slow cooker. These vegetables become tender and sweet when cooked for a long period of time. They can go right into the slow cooker.

More tender vegetables such as mushrooms and bell peppers can be cooked for long periods of time, but they may fall apart. Add them in the last hour or two of cooking time if you prefer a crisp-tender texture.

Here are some additional tips for best results with vegetables.

- Some vegetables, such as onions and garlic, have better flavor if they are precooked. Simply sauté them on the stove top in 1 to 2 teaspoons of olive oil or butter for a few minutes to soften. You can also cook them in the microwave oven in a small amount of butter or olive oil until crisp-tender.
- Caramelized onions add incredible flavor to slow cooker recipes. Cook onions on the stove top in a combination of butter and olive oil until tender. Then lower the heat and cook, stirring frequently, for 20 to 30 minutes until the onions are golden brown. You can freeze these caramelized onions and add them to casseroles, soups, stews, and sauces.
- Hard root vegetables such as potatoes, turnips, and carrots take longer to cook than meats and grains, so place them in the bottom of the slow cooker. When layered in this fashion, juices from the meats will drip down onto the vegetables, adding lots of flavor.
- Tender vegetables such as bell peppers, leafy greens, and peas can be added to the slow cooker toward the end of the cooking time. These ingredients cook to the crisp-tender stage in about one to two hours on low.

How to Cook Grains, Legumes, and Pasta

Adding grains, legumes such as beans or lentils, and pasta to the slow cooker can transform simple recipes into wholesome meals. Rice can go directly into the slow cooker. Legumes must be sorted and rinsed, and should usually be presoaked before cooking. Pasta can be cooked in the slow cooker, provided that it is accompanied by 2 cups of water for each cup or 4 ounces of pasta. You can even make lasagna in the slow cooker!

- Grains cook very well in the slow cooker. Brown rice, converted long-grain rice, and wild rice are the best choices. You can sauté rice for a few minutes in butter to add a toasted flavor to your recipes. Oatmeal and other whole grains such as barley and quinoa are also good choices for the slow cooker.
- Raw legumes such as beans should usually be soaked in cold water before being cooked. Sort the beans and remove extraneous material, then rinse and drain. Place them in a large bowl, add cold water, cover, and let stand overnight. You can also place the beans in a pot, heat them to boiling on the stove top, then cover and let stand for two hours. Drain and use as directed.

- Lentils and split peas do not need to be soaked before cooking. Just sort them, rinse, and drain, and add them directly to the slow cooker.
- You can cook pasta directly in the slow cooker as long as the recipe has enough liquid. Add the pasta during the last 30 minutes of cooking time and stir well. Make sure that the pasta is completely covered with liquid. Check after 20 minutes and stir again. Serve when the pasta is al dente—that is, tender but with a bit of firmness in the center.

SLOW COOKER CLEANUP

Cleaning the slow cooker is easy. Remove all of the food using a rubber spatula or a plastic or wooden spoon so you don't scratch the crockery surface. Make sure the slow cooker liner has cooled. Then place it in the sink and add soap and warm water. If necessary, you can let the slow cooker sit in its water bath for 15 to 20 minutes to loosen the food. Then scrub using a plastic brush (never steel wool) until the liner is clean. Dry it thoroughly, wash the lid, and reassemble the slow cooker.

Cooking bags and foil can help make cleanup even easier. Cooking bags are made of nylon and won't melt in the appliance. When the food is done, pour it out of the bag into the serving dish and just throw the bag away. Voilà!

TEN TIPS FOR COOKING TOGETHER

Cooking should be fun, and sharing this activity can be a wonderful and romantic experience. You will learn a lot about each other as you plan meals, go shopping, cook, eat, and clean up together. While most of these activities are definitely chores, you can make the whole experience fun by following these tips.

1. **Don't cook when you're really hungry.** People tend to get cranky when they're hungry. It's also easier to make mistakes when your blood sugar is low. Snack on some crackers, fresh veggies, or fresh fruit before you start cooking.
2. **Communicate.** The more you talk about what you're doing, the smoother the whole process will be. Tell your partner if you need to use the sink, or if you'd like him or her to pull an ingredient off the shelf for you to use. The more you talk, the more fun the experience will be.
3. **Enjoy the process.** The experience of cooking can be quite sensual. Enjoy the feel of the foods you're handling. Savor the wonderful aromas that waft into the air as you cook. Even the sounds of the kitchen—pasta rattling into a pan, the "thunk" of a knife as it cuts through vegetables or meat, and the sound of food sizzling in a pan—are delicious.
4. **Divide chores.** It's no fun cooking together if one person does the cooking and the other just pulls food out of the pantry! Unless one of you really doesn't enjoys the cooking process, divide the tasks. Even if one of you really enjoys it, you may still share the fun of cooking.
5. **Try something new.** Part of the fun of cooking is learning about new flavors and cuisines. Be adventurous and try some curries from India, or a vegetarian meal if that's new to you.

6. **Be considerate.** Don't snap at your partner if he or she does something wrong. Remember, you're a team! If something drops on the floor, pick it up. If it looks like your partner needs help, be quick to lend a hand.

7. **Work together on cleanup.** Cleaning the kitchen should be a shared process. If one of you washes and the other dries one day, switch those tasks the next day. And try to clean up as you go so you won't be faced with a dirty kitchen after you eat.

8. **Put on music.** Adding music to your time in the kitchen is fun and adds to the romance. Think about matching the music to the food! Put on some Italian opera when you're making risotto, or some American pop music when chili is on the menu.

9. **Learn together.** Remember that you are learning how to cook together. If one of you is interested in a certain cuisine, be enthusiastic. Learn about the culture of the food you're preparing.

10. **Encourage each other.** Be each other's cheerleader! Criticism and bickering have no place in the kitchen. Enjoy every moment you spend together feeding your bodies and souls.

PART TWO

Slow Cooker Recipes for Two

CHAPTER THREE

Eggs and Brunch

When you use a slow cooker to prepare your breakfast the night before, you can wake up the next morning to a delicious meal that's ready to eat. Talk about instant gratification! Most of these breakfast and brunch recipes need to cook for seven to eight hours on low. A programmable slow cooker with a "keep warm" setting can extend that time to nine or ten hours.

Breakfast is the most important meal of the day. Nutrition experts stress that people who eat breakfast tend to weigh less, have fewer health problems, and perform better throughout the day. For that reason, your breakfast should consist of protein, some carbs, fiber, and as many vitamins and minerals as you can pack into the meal.

Whole grains such as oatmeal, barley, and whole-grain breads; eggs; and fruits and vegetables should be the stars of your daily breakfast routine. Those foods will help provide the nutrients you need to get through your day without feeling hungry. And think about adding some more unusual breakfast items from other cuisines to your repertoire. A spicy egg dish from Mexico, like the Mexican Egg Bake, or a hot cereal flavored with curry, like the Curried Oatmeal with Dried Fruit, add interest and wonderful flavor. Egg dishes, stratas, and casserole recipes are delicious for breakfast and work well in the slow cooker. Hot cereals, of course, are a natural for this time-saving appliance.

CURRIED OATMEAL WITH DRIED FRUIT

APPLE BERRY BREAKFAST COBBLER

HONEY WHOLE-GRAIN CEREAL

CARAMEL FRENCH TOAST

CINNAMON STRATA

BACON AND MUSHROOM HASH BROWNS

HAM STRATA

CRUSTLESS QUICHE

EGG AND POTATO CASSEROLE

MEXICAN EGG BAKE

Curried Oatmeal with Dried Fruit

SERVES 2

Prep time: 5 minutes
Cook time: 8 hours

Steel-cut oats are the best variety of oatmeal for the slow cooker because the grains are sturdy and won't fall apart or become mushy. You can find steel-cut oats in any regular grocery store. And remember that curry powders, since they are a blend of different spices, vary in flavor and spiciness from brand to brand. Use more or less curry powder to taste. Pour some cold milk or cream over the hot oatmeal for a satisfying breakfast.

COOKING SPRAY
¾ CUP STEEL-CUT OATS
¼ CUP DRIED CRANBERRIES OR DRIED CHERRIES
¼ CUP GOLDEN RAISINS
½ TO 1 TEASPOON CURRY POWDER
¼ CUP CHOPPED WALNUTS
1 CUP HALF-AND-HALF
1 CUP APPLE JUICE
1 CUP WATER
MILK OR CREAM, CHILLED (OPTIONAL)
BROWN SUGAR (OPTIONAL)

1. Spray the slow cooker with cooking spray.

2. Combine all of the remaining ingredients except the milk and brown sugar in the slow cooker and stir. Cover and cook on low for 7 to 8 hours or until the oatmeal is tender and the liquid has been absorbed.

3. Serve hot with cold milk or cream and some brown sugar sprinkled on top (if using).

Apple Berry Breakfast Cobbler

SERVES 2

Prep time: 20 minutes
Cook time: 8 hours

This cobbler is sweet and tart, made with apples and dried fruit. The topping is tender and moist and slightly crunchy from the pecans. Serve this hearty breakfast warm from the slow cooker with sour cream or unsweetened whipped cream.

COOKING SPRAY

1 CUP ALL-PURPOSE FLOUR, PLUS MORE FOR DUSTING

3 APPLES, PEELED, CORED, AND SLICED

½ CUP DRIED CHERRIES OR CRANBERRIES

1 TABLESPOON FRESHLY SQUEEZED LEMON JUICE

2 TABLESPOONS SUGAR

1 TABLESPOON CORNSTARCH

½ CUP OLD-FASHIONED ROLLED OATS

¼ CUP CHOPPED PECANS

2 TABLESPOONS PACKED BROWN SUGAR

½ TEASPOON GROUND CINNAMON

⅛ TEASPOON GROUND NUTMEG

3 TABLESPOONS UNSALTED BUTTER, MELTED

SOUR CREAM OR LIGHT WHIPPED CREAM (OPTIONAL)

1. Spray the slow cooker with cooking spray and dust with flour. Tap out any excess flour from the insert.

2. Place the apples and cherries into the slow cooker and sprinkle with the lemon juice, sugar, and cornstarch; toss to combine.

3. In a small bowl, combine the 1 cup of flour, oats, pecans, brown sugar, cinnamon, and nutmeg and mix well. Add the melted butter and stir until crumbly. Sprinkle the mixture on top of the fruit.

4. Cover and cook on low for 7 to 8 hours or until the apples are tender when pierced with a fork. Serve with sour cream or light whipped cream (if using).

Honey Whole-Grain Cereal

SERVES 2

Prep time: 5 minutes
Cook time: 8 hours

Whole grains cook beautifully in the slow cooker. Oatmeal is delicious for breakfast, of course, but why not try other grains, too? This combination of barley and wild rice is nutty and flavorful, with the most wonderful texture. Honey and spices are perfect ingredients to add interest. Serve with cold whole milk and some brown sugar, maple syrup, or honey on top.

½ CUP WILD RICE, RINSED AND DRAINED
½ CUP PEARL BARLEY, RINSED AND DRAINED
1½ CUP APPLE JUICE OR PEAR NECTAR
1 CUP WATER
3 TABLESPOONS HONEY
½ TEASPOON GROUND CINNAMON
⅛ TEASPOON GROUND NUTMEG
DASH OF SALT
WHOLE MILK, CHILLED (OPTIONAL)
MAPLE SYRUP, HONEY, OR BROWN SUGAR (OPTIONAL)

1. Combine all of the ingredients except the milk and maple syrup in the slow cooker and stir. Cover and cook on low for 7 to 8 hours or until the wild rice and barley are tender.

2. Stir and serve with milk and maple syrup, honey, or brown sugar (if using).

Caramel French Toast

Prep time: 15 minutes
Cook time: 2 hours

This recipe cooks in only two hours on high heat, so it's perfect for a leisurely brunch. Let it cook while you read the paper and sip some coffee. The bread becomes light and fluffy and almost creamy in this delicious dish, and the caramel sauce adds wonderful flavor.

COOKING SPRAY
ALL-PURPOSE FLOUR
3 CUPS CUBED FRENCH BREAD OR CHALLAH
2 EGGS, BEATEN
⅔ CUP WHOLE MILK
1 TABLESPOON GRANULATED SUGAR
½ TEASPOON GROUND CINNAMON
2 TABLESPOONS UNSALTED BUTTER, MELTED
3 TABLESPOONS PACKED BROWN SUGAR
1 TABLESPOON HONEY
¼ CUP CHOPPED PECANS
MAPLE SYRUP OR SOUR CREAM (OPTIONAL)

1. Spray the slow cooker with cooking spray, and dust with flour. Tap out any excess flour from the insert, and add the bread cubes.

2. In a small bowl, combine the eggs, milk, granulated sugar, and ¼ teaspoon of the cinnamon. In another small bowl, combine the melted butter, brown sugar, honey, and remaining ¼ teaspoon of cinnamon.

3. Pour the egg mixture over the bread and let stand for 5 minutes. Then drizzle the bread with the brown sugar mixture and sprinkle with the pecans.

4. Cover and cook on high for 1½ to 2 hours, or until an instant-read thermometer registers 165°F. Serve warm with maple syrup or sour cream (if using).

Cinnamon Strata

Prep time: 10 minutes
Cook time: 2 hours

Stratas, are usually savory, made with herbs and meats, so this sweet version is a nice change of pace. The cinnamon gives it a warm flavor and a tantalizing aroma. The crisp topping, added just before serving, is a wonderful textural contrast.

COOKING SPRAY
5 SLICES CINNAMON BREAD, CUT INTO CUBES
⅓ CUP GOLDEN RAISINS
3 EGGS, BEATEN
⅔ CUP WHOLE MILK
1 TABLESPOON PACKED BROWN SUGAR
¼ TEASPOON PURE VANILLA EXTRACT
½ TEASPOON GROUND CINNAMON
PINCH OF SALT
½ CUP CINNAMON-FLAVORED GRANOLA
MAPLE SYRUP (OPTIONAL)

1. Spray the slow cooker with cooking spray. Combine the bread cubes and the raisins in the slow cooker; toss gently to mix.

2. In a small bowl, combine the eggs, milk, brown sugar, vanilla, cinnamon, and salt and beat well. Pour into the slow cooker. Let stand for 5 minutes, gently pressing the bread into the egg occasionally so it absorbs the mixture.

3. Cover and cook on high for 2 hours, or until an instant-read thermometer registers 165°F. Top each serving with cinnamon granola. Drizzle with maple syrup (if using).

Bacon and Mushroom Hash Browns

Prep time: 20 minutes
Cook time: 7 hours

Frozen hash brown potatoes cook beautifully in the slow cooker. When paired with crisp bacon, gooey cheese, and some flavorful mushrooms, this delicious casserole makes a hearty and satisfying breakfast.

COOKING SPRAY
3 SLICES BACON
½ CUP CHOPPED ONION
1 GARLIC CLOVE, MINCED
6 BUTTON MUSHROOMS, SLICED
3 CUPS FROZEN HASH BROWN POTATOES
1 CUP PREPARED ALFREDO SAUCE (FROM A 16-OUNCE JAR)
1 CUP SHREDDED COLBY CHEESE
¼ CUP CHOPPED FRESH PARSLEY LEAVES
SOUR CREAM (OPTIONAL)

1. Line the slow cooker with foil and spray with cooking spray. In a small skillet over medium heat, cook the bacon until crisp. Using a slotted spoon, remove the bacon from the skillet and transfer it to a plate lined with paper towels to drain. Crumble the bacon and set it aside.

2. In the drippings remaining in the skillet, cook the onion and garlic over medium heat until translucent, 4 to 5 minutes. Add the mushrooms and cook for 2 to 3 minutes longer, until they are almost tender.

3. Combine the bacon, onion, garlic, mushrooms, and potatoes in the slow cooker and stir to mix. Add the Alfredo sauce and cheese and stir gently.

4. Cover and cook on low for 6 to 7 hours until the potatoes are tender. Sprinkle with parsley and serve with sour cream (if using).

Ham Strata

Prep time: 15 minutes
Cook time: 6 hours

A strata is made of bread layered with other ingredients, soaked in an egg and milk mixture and cooked until puffy. Stratas are usually baked in the oven, but they cook very well in the slow cooker. You can swap out the Swiss or Gruyère cheese for your favorite type of cheese in this easy recipe. Vary the type of meat, too; you can use smoked ham, prosciutto, or ordinary canned ham.

COOKING SPRAY

3 CUPS CUBED TOASTED FRENCH BREAD

⅔ CUP CUBED FULLY COOKED HAM

1 CUP SHREDDED SWISS OR GRUYÈRE CHEESE

¼ CUP SLICED GREEN ONIONS, WHITE AND GREEN PARTS

3 EGGS, BEATEN

¾ CUP WHOLE MILK

2 TEASPOONS DIJON MUSTARD

⅛ TEASPOON SALT

FRESHLY GROUND BLACK PEPPER

¼ TEASPOON DRIED THYME

1. Spray the slow cooker with cooking spray. Layer the bread, ham, cheese, and green onions in the slow cooker.

2. In a small bowl, combine the eggs, milk, mustard, salt, pepper, and thyme and mix well. Pour the egg mixture into the slow cooker. Let stand for 5 minutes, occasionally pressing the bread into the egg so it absorbs the mixture.

3. Cover and cook on low for 5 to 6 hours, until an instant-read thermometer registers 165°F.

Crustless Quiche

Prep time: 15 minutes
Cook time: 2 hours

A quiche is just a mixture of eggs, cream, cheese, and other ingredients such as meats or vegetables poured into a pastry shell and baked until puffy. But the moist heat of the slow cooker would ruin a crust, which needs dry heat to cook properly, so the crisp bread crumbs added just before serving mimic this texture.

Panko bread crumbs are larger and much crisper than ordinary bread crumbs and have tiny sharp corners. You can find them in the grocery store, packaged in boxes, next to the regular Italian bread crumbs. You can substitute regular dried bread crumbs for panko bread crumbs in most recipes, including this one.

COOKING SPRAY
½ POUND FRESH SAUSAGE, CASINGS REMOVED
½ CUP CHOPPED ONION
½ CUP CHOPPED RED BELL PEPPER
1 CUP SHREDDED MONTEREY JACK CHEESE
5 EGGS, BEATEN
⅔ CUP LIGHT CREAM
2 TABLESPOONS ALL-PURPOSE FLOUR
⅛ TEASPOON SALT
FRESHLY GROUND BLACK PEPPER
1 TABLESPOON UNSALTED BUTTER
⅔ CUP PANKO BREAD CRUMBS

1. Line the slow cooker with foil and spray with cooking spray.

2. In a small skillet, cook the sausage with the onion, stirring to break up the meat, until the sausage is thoroughly cooked. Add the bell pepper and cook for 2 minutes. Drain well.

continued ▶

3. Place the sausage, onion, and bell pepper in the slow cooker and top with the cheese.

4. In a small bowl, beat together the eggs, cream, flour, salt, and black pepper. Pour the mixture into the slow cooker. Cover and cook on high for 2 hours or until an instant-read thermometer registers 165°F.

5. Meanwhile, melt the butter in a small skillet and add the bread crumbs; cook and stir over medium heat until the bread crumbs are toasted.

6. Cut the quiche into wedges. Top with the toasted bread crumbs just before serving.

Egg and Potato Casserole

SERVES 2

Prep time: 15 minutes
Cook time: 8 hours

When you want a warm and comforting breakfast, this is the recipe to make. Tender potatoes, creamy eggs, and melted cheese combine to make a superb meal. Vary the cheese to use your favorite. And don't be afraid to experiment with herbs—thyme, basil, and oregano would all be delicious.

You can add cooked meats to almost any slow cooker egg recipe. Try crisply cooked bacon, drained and crumbled; cooked sausage; frozen meatless crumbles; or leftover cooked chicken, shrimp, or pork. Just stir the prepared meat into the egg mixture and pour it into the slow cooker. Cover and cook as directed in the recipe.

COOKING SPRAY

⅓ CUP WHOLE MILK

1 OUNCE CREAM CHEESE, CUT INTO CUBES

3 EGGS

½ TEASPOON DRIED MARJORAM

⅛ TEASPOON SALT

FRESHLY GROUND BLACK PEPPER

3½ CUPS FROZEN HASH BROWN POTATOES

1 CUP SHREDDED MONTEREY JACK CHEESE

2 TABLESPOONS GRATED PARMESAN CHEESE

1. Spray the slow cooker with cooking spray.

2. In a small microwave-safe bowl, combine the milk and cream cheese. Microwave on high for 1 minute; remove and stir until blended. Let cool for 5 minutes, then beat in the eggs, marjoram, salt, and black pepper.

continued ▶

3. Layer the hash brown potatoes and Monterey Jack cheese in the slow cooker. Pour the egg mixture over all, and then sprinkle with the Parmesan cheese.

4. Cover and cook on low for 7 to 8 hours or until the potatoes are tender and an instant-read thermometer registers 165°F.

5. Scoop the casserole into individual bowls and serve hot.

Mexican Egg Bake

SERVES 2

Prep time: 20 minutes
Cook time: 7 hours

This recipe will wake you up! Just remember that you can make this dish as spicy or as mild as you'd like. If you like hot foods, add another jalapeño pepper or use a hotter pepper, such as habanero or Scotch bonnet. Milder peppers include poblano peppers and green bell peppers.

Use this recipe to make breakfast burritos. Just spoon the egg mixture onto warmed flour or corn tortillas; add some salsa, chopped avocados, or sour cream; then roll up and enjoy. If you have leftovers, store them, covered, in the refrigerator within two hours. You can reheat this dish in the microwave, cooking on high for 1 to 2 minutes until steaming.

COOKING SPRAY
½ POUND CHORIZO SAUSAGE, CASINGS REMOVED
½ CUP CHOPPED ONION
1 GARLIC CLOVE, MINCED
⅓ CUP CHOPPED RED BELL PEPPER
½ JALAPEÑO PEPPER, MINCED
4 EGGS
¼ CUP WHOLE MILK
⅓ CUP SALSA
¼ TEASPOON DRIED OREGANO
½ CUP SHREDDED PEPPER JACK CHEESE

1. Spray a slow cooker with cooking spray. In a small skillet, cook the sausage with the onion and garlic over medium heat, stirring to break up the meat, until the sausage is browned, about 5 minutes. Drain well.

2. Place the sausage, onion, garlic, bell pepper, and jalapeño pepper in the slow cooker.

3. In a small bowl, beat the eggs with the milk, salsa, and oregano. Pour the mixture into the slow cooker.

4. Cover and cook on low for 6 to 7 hours or until the eggs are set and an instant-read thermometer registers 165°F. Top with the cheese, cover, and let stand for 5 minutes before serving.

CHAPTER FOUR

Sauces, Dips, and Appetizers

Even when it's just the two of you, sometimes you want a dinner with several courses. Enter the slow cooker. In this handy appliance, dips and starters come together effortlessly to complement your meals, and luscious sauces are made to transform anything from pasta to meats, vegetables, and fruits. If you're craving a light dinner, choose a dip served with vegetables and two or three heartier appetizers, along with a green salad and some crusty bread.

If you're entertaining, you can double or triple the dip recipes in this chapter and cook them in a larger slow cooker, and then use your trusty smaller slow cooker to keep appetizer dips warm while your guests are chatting.

The appetizer recipes can also be used in other ways. For instance, use leftover Buffalo Chicken Meatballs to make a delicious meatball sandwich the next day. You can also use French Onion Dip as a sandwich spread, or thin it out with a little milk, white wine, or chicken broth and serve it over pasta. The possibilities are endless!

CINNAMON APPLESAUCE

ROASTED TOMATO MARINARA SAUCE

BARBECUE SAUCE

CHILE CON QUESO

PIZZA DIP

FRENCH ONION DIP

ARTICHOKE CRAB DIP

WHITE BEAN AND TOMATO DIP

TEX-MEX FONDUE

CURRIED MEATBALLS

STUFFED MUSHROOMS

BUFFALO CHICKEN MEATBALLS

GARLIC SHRIMP

SPICY SWEET NUT MIX

BBQ CHICKEN WINGS

Cinnamon Applesauce

MAKES 4 CUPS

Prep time: 10 minutes
Cook time: 7 hours

The best apples to use in this recipe are cooking apples such as Cortland, Fuji, Granny Smith, Gravenstein, Jonagold, McIntosh, Rome Beauty, and Winesap. These apples have a firm texture and sweet-tart flavor that stands up to heat. Depending on the tartness of the apples, you can cut the sugar amount in half if you'd like. Very little liquid is used in this recipe because the apples give off juice as they cook. You can freeze leftover applesauce for up to three months; thaw it in the refrigerator.

1½ POUNDS APPLES, PEELED, CORED, AND SLICED
2 TABLESPOONS FRESHLY SQUEEZED LEMON JUICE
3 TABLESPOONS PACKED LIGHT BROWN SUGAR
PINCH OF SALT
½ TEASPOON GROUND CINNAMON
¼ TEASPOON APPLE PIE SPICE

1. Combine all the ingredients in the slow cooker and stir.

2. Cover and cook on low for 6 to 7 hours. After 4 hours, check the mixture and stir. If you like chunky applesauce, you may want to stop the cooking process at this point. If you like smooth applesauce, cook for the full time. Stir or mash the apples until the sauce reaches your desired consistency. You can also use an immersion blender to process the mixture until smooth.

Roasted Tomato Marinara Sauce

MAKES 4 CUPS

Prep time: 20 minutes
Cook time: 7 hours

Roasting tomatoes before cooking the sauce adds a wonderful smoky flavor to this classic recipe. You can also omit this step for a classic marinara. This sauce freezes very well. Spoon it into 1-cup freezer bags or containers, then seal, label, and freeze it for up to six months. To use, empty the container into a saucepan and heat until simmering.

Tomato paste is usually sold in 6-ounce cans. Since many recipes do not call for the whole can, that can mean a lot of waste. There are a few ways to solve this problem. You can remove the paste from the can and freeze it in 1-tablespoon dollops; use from the freezer as needed. Or you can buy tomato paste in a squeeze tube and store it in the refrigerator.

12 ROMA OR PLUM TOMATOES
1 SMALL ONION, CHOPPED
1 TABLESPOON EXTRA-VIRGIN OLIVE OIL
½ TEASPOON SALT
2 GARLIC CLOVES, MINCED
2 TABLESPOONS TOMATO PASTE
½ TEASPOON DRIED ITALIAN SEASONING
1 TABLESPOON RED WINE VINEGAR

1. Preheat the oven to 400°F.

2. Place the tomatoes and onion on a rimmed baking sheet and drizzle with the olive oil; sprinkle with the salt. Roast the vegetables for 30 minutes or until the tomatoes start to brown a bit.

3. Combine the tomatoes, onion, and any juice in the slow cooker along with the remaining ingredients. Cover and cook on low for 6 to 7 hours or until the sauce is blended and fragrant.

4. At this point, taste the sauce and add more salt and Italian seasoning as needed. For a smoother texture, you can use an immersion blender to purée the sauce right in the slow cooker, or you can transfer it carefully to a blender and purée. Spoon the sauce into containers and refrigerate up to 4 days, or freeze for up to 6 months.

Barbecue Sauce

MAKES 4 CUPS

Prep time: 15 minutes
Cook time: 7 hours

Making your own homemade barbecue sauce is something special. This recipe is so flexible that you can change the seasonings and spices to include your favorites. If you like milder food, omit the red pepper flakes and use less chili powder. If you like your BBQ spicy, the sky's the limit! Just make sure to taste as you season. Brush this on chicken, pork, lamb, or beef as you grill.

1½ CUPS KETCHUP

½ CUP PACKED BROWN SUGAR

¼ CUP MOLASSES

¼ CUP TOMATO PASTE

¼ CUP RED WINE VINEGAR

3 TABLESPOONS DIJON MUSTARD

¼ CUP WATER

1 CUP MINCED ONION

2 CLOVES GARLIC, MINCED

1 TEASPOON SMOKED PAPRIKA

¼ TEASPOON CELERY SALT

1 TO 2 TEASPOONS CHILI POWDER

¼ TEASPOON RED PEPPER FLAKES

½ TEASPOON SALT

⅛ TEASPOON FRESHLY GROUND BLACK PEPPER

1. Combine all ingredients in the slow cooker and stir to blend well. Cover and cook on low for 5 to 7 hours or until the sauce tastes rich and blended.

2. Cover and refrigerate for up to 1 week, or freeze for up to 3 months. Thaw the sauce in the refrigerator and reheat before using.

Chile con Queso

Prep time: 15 minutes
Cook time: 2½ hours

This classic appetizer dip is perfect for Cinco de Mayo celebrations or for whenever you are serving Mexican food. It's one of the few recipes in this book that uses processed cheese, but for good reason. When making a cheese sauce, you need the emulsifiers and other ingredients in that product so the cheese doesn't break down as it heats, which would make the sauce lumpy. Serve this sauce straight from the slow cooker to keep it warm, and pair it with tortilla chips and lots of veggies for dipping. You can also use it as a topping for burritos or enchiladas, or freeze leftovers for later use.

2 TABLESPOONS UNSALTED BUTTER
1 CUP DICED ONION
2 GARLIC CLOVES, MINCED
1 CUP SHREDDED MONTEREY JACK CHEESE
2 CUPS SHREDDED WHITE AMERICAN PROCESSED CHEESE
1 CUP GRATED COTIJA CHEESE
½ CUP WHOLE MILK
1 SMALL JALAPEÑO PEPPER, MINCED
1 SMALL TOMATO, CHOPPED
A FEW DROPS OF HOT SAUCE (OPTIONAL)

1. In a small skillet over medium heat, melt the butter and cook the onion and garlic until tender, 5 to 6 minutes.

2. Combine the onion mixture and remaining ingredients in the slow cooker and stir. Cover and cook on low for 2 to 2½ hours, stirring once during the cooking time, until the cheese is melted and the dip is smooth. Serve immediately.

Pizza Dip

Prep time: 15 minutes
Cook time: 3 hours

This is like eating a pizza in dip form! It's creamy and slightly spicy. Serve it with crisp or chewy breadsticks for dipping, or toast some French bread slices and spread the dip on them. Freeze leftovers; reheat and use as a quesadilla filling or pasta sauce.

ONE 8-OUNCE PACKAGE CREAM CHEESE, AT ROOM TEMPERATURE
1 CUP PREPARED PIZZA SAUCE
10 CHERRY TOMATOES, CHOPPED
3 TABLESPOONS CHOPPED GREEN ONIONS, WHITE AND GREEN PARTS
⅛ TEASPOON GARLIC POWDER
¼ TEASPOON DRIED ITALIAN SEASONING
1 CUP SHREDDED MOZZARELLA CHEESE
½ CUP PEPPERONI SLICES

1. Combine all of the ingredients in the slow cooker and stir gently.

2. Cover and cook on low for 2 to 3 hours or until the cheese has melted, stirring once halfway through the cooking time. Serve right from the slow cooker with dippers.

French Onion Dip

Prep time: 15 minutes
Cook time: 11½ hours

This delicious and rich recipe was inspired by classic French onion soup. The onions are caramelized in the slow cooker before the rest of the ingredients are added. Serve this dip with toasted French bread to mimic the classic topping for the soup. It is also delicious served with crudités such as baby carrots, slices of bell peppers, cauliflower, and broccoli, and it freezes well.

Caramelized onions are a wonderful addition to many recipes. Double or triple the caramelized onion portion of this recipe, then freeze the onions in ½-cup portions. Add them to chicken soup, marinara sauce, risotto, pilafs, or casseroles. The onions can be frozen for up to six months. You can add some chopped or minced garlic to the onions after they are partially cooked for even more flavor.

2 ONIONS, THINLY SLICED
2 TABLESPOONS EXTRA-VIRGIN OLIVE OIL
1 TABLESPOON UNSALTED BUTTER
¼ TEASPOON SALT
2 GARLIC CLOVES, MINCED
½ CUP LOW-SODIUM BEEF BROTH
½ TEASPOON DRIED THYME
ONE 3-OUNCE PACKAGE CREAM CHEESE, AT ROOM TEMPERATURE
1 CUP SOUR CREAM
1½ CUPS GRATED GRUYÈRE OR SWISS CHEESE
1 TABLESPOON CORNSTARCH

1. Combine the onions, olive oil, butter, and salt in the slow cooker. Cover and cook on high for 8 to 9 hours or until the onions turn golden brown. You can stir once or twice during the cooking time. This step can be done ahead of time; refrigerate the cooked onions until you are ready to make the dip.

2. Combine the onions with the remaining ingredients in the slow cooker. Cover and cook on low for 2 to 2½ hours or until the mixture is smooth and creamy. Stir gently and serve immediately.

Artichoke and Crab Dip

Prep time: 15 minutes
Cook time: 3 hours

Artichoke dip is a classic slow cooker recipe. Add some crab to this dish to elevate it to another level. This is one of the bonuses of cooking for two: You can afford to splurge on a small amount of luxury ingredients every once in a while. You can substitute an equal amount of shrimp for the crab if you'd like. Serve this dip with breadsticks or toasted French bread.

COOKING SPRAY
2 CUPS FROZEN ARTICHOKE HEARTS, THAWED AND DRAINED
TWO 3-OUNCE PACKAGE CREAM CHEESE, AT ROOM TEMPERATURE
½ CUP MAYONNAISE
1 CUP PASTEURIZED CRAB MEAT, DRAINED AND PICKED OVER
1 GARLIC CLOVE, MINCED
¼ CUP CHOPPED GREEN ONIONS, WHITE AND GREEN PARTS
1 CUP GRATED HAVARTI CHEESE
1 TABLESPOON FRESHLY SQUEEZED LEMON JUICE

1. Spray the slow cooker with cooking spray. Combine all of the remaining ingredients in the slow cooker and stir.

2. Cover and cook on low for 2 to 3 hours or until the cheese is melted. Stir to combine and serve immediately.

White Bean and Tomato Dip

MAKES 4 CUPS

Prep time: 10 minutes
Cook time: 8 hours

White beans make a creamy dip with very little fat. Paired with sweet and tangy sun-dried tomatoes, this dip is satisfying but not heavy. Serve it with endive leaves, bell pepper strips, and pita chips. Freeze leftovers in a hard sided container; thaw and reheat on the stovetop to serve another time.

1 CUP DRIED WHITE BEANS, SORTED AND RINSED

3 GARLIC CLOVES, PEELED

3 CUPS WATER

1 TABLESPOON EXTRA-VIRGIN OLIVE OIL

⅔ CUP SOUR CREAM

2 TABLESPOONS FRESHLY SQUEEZED LEMON JUICE

3 TABLESPOONS GRATED PARMESAN CHEESE

½ TEASPOON SALT

PINCH OF FRESHLY GROUND BLACK PEPPER

3 TABLESPOONS MINCED SUN-DRIED TOMATOES

½ TEASPOON DRIED THYME

1. Combine the beans and garlic in the slow cooker, and pour in the water. Cover and cook on low for 7 to 8 hours or until the beans are tender.

2. Drain the beans and place them in a food processor with the olive oil, sour cream, lemon juice, cheese, salt, and pepper. Process until smooth. Place the bean mixture in a bowl and stir in the tomatoes and thyme. Serve immediately or cover and chill for a few hours before serving.

Tex-Mex Fondue

SERVES 2

Prep time: 10 minutes
Cook time: 4 hours

Fondue cooks beautifully in the slow cooker. The cheese should melt slowly to prevent burning and to ensure that it combines smoothly with the other ingredients. Tex-Mex food is a combination of Mexican cuisine and the foods of the Southwest. This spicy and rich fondue is delicious served with cooked sausages, toasted corn bread cubes, cherry tomatoes, and red bell peppers for dipping. Freeze leftovers to use in burritos or tacos.

2 TABLESPOONS UNSALTED BUTTER

½ CUP MINCED ONION

1 GARLIC CLOVE, MINCED

½ SMALL JALAPEÑO PEPPER, MINCED

1 CUP LAGER BEER

1½ CUPS SHREDDED SWISS CHEESE

1½ CUPS SHREDDED MONTEREY JACK CHEESE

½ CUP CRUMBLED QUESO FRESCO CHEESE

2 TABLESPOONS ALL-PURPOSE FLOUR

1 TABLESPOON CHOPPED FRESH CILANTRO LEAVES

1. In a small saucepan, heat the butter over medium heat. Add the onion and garlic; cook and stir until translucent, about 3 minutes. Add the jalapeño and cook for another minute. Place the mixture in the slow cooker.

2. Stir in the beer; cover and cook on low for 2 hours or until the mixture is hot.

3. In a small bowl, toss the cheeses with the flour. Add the cheese mixture to the slow cooker and stir. Cover and cook on low for 1 to 2 hours longer, stirring once after about 45 minutes, until the cheese is melted and the mixture is smooth. Sprinkle with cilantro and serve immediately.

Curried Meatballs

Prep time: 10 minutes
Cook time: 4 hours

Frozen precooked meatballs are one of the best convenience foods around. They are made in many flavors, including classic Italian, pesto, and wild rice. You can even find precooked chicken meatballs. For this recipe, choose a plain variety. Serve the meatballs with little toothpicks or with small plates and forks. Leftovers are delicious in sandwiches.

15 FROZEN PRECOOKED MEATBALLS
½ CUP PEACH PRESERVES
⅓ CUP MANGO CHUTNEY
3 TABLESPOONS PINEAPPLE JUICE
2 TABLESPOONS PACKED BROWN SUGAR
1 TEASPOON CURRY POWDER

1. Combine all ingredients in the slow cooker and stir gently.

2. Cover and cook on high for 4 hours, or until the meatballs are hot and an instant-read thermometer registers 165°F. Serve immediately.

Stuffed Mushrooms

SERVES 2

Prep time: 20 minutes
Cook time: 2 hours

Stuffed mushrooms are the perfect appetizer for a special occasion. You can stuff them with anything you like, but this flavorful recipe is a good starting point. In the supermarket, you can usually find large button mushrooms, which are best for stuffing. You can use portobello mushrooms, too, if you prefer.

Mushrooms are grown covered in soil, so they must be cleaned before you can eat them. But don't worry—the dirt is sterile! Don't soak mushrooms in water to clean, or they will soak up all that liquid and become mushy. Instead, quickly rinse them under cool running water and use your fingers to brush off any soil. Mushrooms are quite perishable. Store them in the fridge and use them within three days.

6 LARGE MUSHROOMS
1 TABLESPOON UNSALTED BUTTER
2 TEASPOONS EXTRA-VIRGIN OLIVE OIL
5 TABLESPOONS FINELY MINCED ONION
1 GARLIC CLOVE, MINCED
½ CUP SOFT BREAD CRUMBS
¾ CUP SHREDDED GRUYÈRE CHEESE
1 TABLESPOON GRATED PARMESAN CHEESE
⅛ TEASPOON SALT
¼ TEASPOON DRIED OREGANO

1. Remove the stems from the mushrooms and set the caps aside. Trim off the ends of the stems and chop the stems into small pieces.

2. In a small saucepan, heat the butter and olive oil over medium heat. Add the chopped mushroom stems, onion, and garlic and cook until tender, 4 to 5 minutes. Remove the pan from the heat.

3. In a small bowl, combine the cooked vegetables, bread crumbs, cheeses, salt, and oregano. Stuff this mixture into the mushroom caps. Arrange the mushrooms stuffing-side up in the bottom of the slow cooker.

4. Cover and cook on high for 2 hours or until the mushrooms are tender and the cheese has melted. Serve immediately.

Buffalo Chicken Meatballs

Prep time: 20 minutes
Cook time: 4 hours

The Buffalo flavor comes from the famous Buffalo chicken wings served at the Anchor Bar in New York. The wings are broiled and coated in hot sauce, then served with a blue cheese dip and celery sticks. In this recipe, ground chicken is mixed with bread crumbs, blue cheese, and chopped celery, then cooked to tender perfection in hot sauce. A creamy blue cheese dip is the perfect finishing touch.

1 TABLESPOON UNSALTED BUTTER

3 TABLESPOONS FINELY CHOPPED ONION

3 TABLESPOONS FINELY CHOPPED CELERY

3 TABLESPOONS SOFT BREAD CRUMBS

A FEW DROPS TABASCO SAUCE

4 TABLESPOONS CRUMBLED BLUE CHEESE

1 EGG WHITE

½ POUND GROUND CHICKEN

2 TABLESPOONS EXTRA-VIRGIN OLIVE OIL

½ CUP BUFFALO HOT WING SAUCE

3 TABLESPOONS LOW-SODIUM CHICKEN BROTH

½ CUP SOUR CREAM

1. In a small saucepan, melt the butter over medium heat. Add the onion and celery and cook until tender, 4 to 5 minutes. Remove the pan from the heat and place the vegetables in a small bowl. Let cool for 5 minutes.

2. Add the bread crumbs, Tabasco sauce, 2 tablespoons of the blue cheese, and the egg white to the bowl with the vegetables and mix well. Add the ground chicken and mix with your hands until blended. Form the mixture into 1-inch meatballs.

3. In a medium nonstick skillet over medium-high heat, heat the olive oil. Add the meatballs and brown for 1 to 2 minutes on each side; do not cook through. As the meatballs are browned, add them to the slow cooker.

4. In a small bowl, combine the hot wing sauce and chicken broth. Pour the mixture over the meatballs in the slow cooker.

5. Cover and cook on low for 3-4 hours, or until the meatballs register 165°F on an instant-read thermometer.

6. In a small bowl, combine the sour cream and the remaining 2 tablespoons of blue cheese. Serve with the meatballs.

Garlic Shrimp

SERVES 2

Prep time: 5 minutes
Cook time: 45 minutes

If you love shrimp, this is the recipe for you! And if you're also a big fan of garlic, go ahead and add a few more cloves. As they cook with the shrimp, the garlic cloves will become soft and sweet, losing much of their heat and bite. This recipe can be doubled and cooked in a 3-quart slow cooker for a main dish; serve the garlicky shrimp hot over cooked brown rice or hot cooked pasta.

¼ CUP EXTRA-VIRGIN OLIVE OIL

2 TABLESPOONS UNSALTED BUTTER

3 GARLIC CLOVES, SLICED

1 POUND UNCOOKED SHRIMP, PEELED AND DEVEINED

2 TABLESPOONS FRESHLY SQUEEZED LEMON JUICE

⅛ TEASPOON SALT

PINCH OF FRESHLY GROUND BLACK PEPPER

2 TABLESPOONS CHOPPED FRESH BASIL LEAVES

1. Combine the olive oil, butter, and garlic in the slow cooker. Cover and cook on high for 30 minutes.

2. Stir in the shrimp, lemon juice, salt, and pepper and cover. Cook on high for 10 to 15 minutes or until the shrimp curl and turn pink. Sprinkle with basil and serve immediately.

Spicy-Sweet Nut Mix

MAKES 5 CUPS

Prep time: 5 minutes
Cook time: 4 hours

A snack mix is just the thing to have on hand when you're watching a game on television or hosting an impromptu get-together. You can vary this recipe any way you'd like. Change the nuts, add more spices, or add different snack foods. This is an unusual slow cooker recipe in that it is cooked uncovered, and you do have to stir the mixture every 30 minutes. But that's easy!

2 CUPS BITE-SIZE SQUARE GRAIN CEREAL
1 CUP MINI PRETZELS
1 CUP WHOLE PECANS
½ CUP CASHEWS
½ CUP PISTACHIOS
¼ CUP UNSALTED BUTTER, MELTED
3 TABLESPOONS PACKED BROWN SUGAR
2 TEASPOONS CHILI POWDER
⅛ TEASPOON SALT

1. Combine all of the ingredients in the slow cooker. Stir gently.

2. Leave the cover off. Cook on high for 2 hours, stirring the mixture from the bottom every 30 minutes, then cook on low for 2 hours longer without stirring.

3. Remove the snack mix from the slow cooker and spread it on a cookie sheet. Let the mixture cool completely before serving. Store in an airtight container at room temperature for up to a week.

BBQ Chicken Wings

Prep time: 5 minutes
Cook time: 5 hours

These chicken wings must be broiled before you put them in the slow cooker, otherwise the skin will be flabby and unappetizing. Watch them carefully as they brown. You can buy whole chicken wings and disjoint them yourself, or you can buy a product called "chicken drummies," which are the large upper portion of the wing.

1½ POUNDS WHOLE CHICKEN WINGS OR 1 POUND CHICKEN DRUMMIES

¾ CUP BARBECUE SAUCE (SEE PAGE 38)

2 TABLESPOONS HONEY

1 TABLESPOON DIJON MUSTARD

1 TABLESPOON SOY SAUCE

1. If you purchased whole chicken wings, cut off and discard the wing tips. Cut the remaining wing into two pieces. If you purchased chicken drummies, you don't need to do anything.

2. Preheat the broiler to high.

3. Place the chicken on a broiler pan. Broil the chicken 4 to 5 inches from the heat source for about 8 to 9 minutes on each side, turning once, until the wings are golden brown.

4. Meanwhile, combine the remaining ingredients in the slow cooker and stir.

5. When the chicken wings are browned, stir them into the sauce in the slow cooker. Cover and cook on low for 4½ to 5 hours, until the chicken reaches 160°F on an instant-read thermometer. Serve hot.

CHAPTER FIVE

Soups, Stews, and Chilies

The differences between soups, stews, and chilies lie in their textures and ingredients. Soups are thinner, made with unthickened broth or stock. Stews are thicker, usually made with cornstarch, flour, or puréed vegetables to change the texture. And chilies are made with spicy ingredients, meats, beans, and vegetables. Since they all benefit from long cooking times and are easily halved or doubled, these meal-in-a-bowl recipes are naturals for slow cookers of all sizes.

Hearty, healthful, and comforting, these are the meals you crave on cold, snowy days. In fact, scientific research has proven that chicken soup can actually help you feel better when you are sick. A compound in chicken soup called carnosine helps your body's immune system fight viruses, and the other ingredients, such as carrots and onions, are packed with nutrients to help improve your health.

Soups, stews, and chilies are also very forgiving to the novice cook, and they easily accommodate substitutions. No matter what you'd like to alter in one of these recipes—use a different meat or bean, add more vegetables, change the type of vegetables, change the seasoning and spices—the result will be delicious (as long as you taste the seasonings as you go). So enjoy these delicious recipes and have fun experimenting. Just make sure you write down the concoctions you create. Soups and stews can be different every time you make them. That's part of the fun of cooking!

Lentil Soup

SERVES 2

Prep time: 15 minutes
Cook time: 8 hours

Lentil soup is a classic recipe for the slow cooker. For meat lovers, you can add diced ham or some cooked crumbled bacon. The tomato and lemon juice are stirred in at the end because those acidic ingredients would prevent the lentils from softening in the liquid.

¾ CUP DRIED LENTILS

3½ CUPS WATER OR LOW-SODIUM VEGETABLE BROTH

½ CUP MINCED ONION

1 GARLIC CLOVE, MINCED

½ CUP CHOPPED CARROT

½ CUP CHOPPED CELERY

½ TEASPOON DRIED BASIL

½ TEASPOON SALT

1 TOMATO, CHOPPED

1 TABLESPOON FRESHLY SQUEEZED LEMON JUICE

1. Pick over the lentils to remove any shriveled legumes or extraneous material. Rinse the lentils and drain them in a colander.

2. In the slow cooker, combine the lentils, water, onion, garlic, carrot, celery, and basil. Cover and cook on low for 5 to 6 hours or until the lentils are tender.

3. Stir in the salt, tomato, and lemon juice. Cover and cook on low for 1 to 2 hours longer or until the flavors have melded. Serve hot.

Chicken Noodle Soup

SERVES 2

Prep time: 20 minutes
Cook time: 7 hours

This recipe is so comforting and very good for you. Chicken thighs are used in this soup because they are more tender than breasts and never overcook in the slow cooker. You can add any type of herb or spice you'd like, or change the vegetables.

½ CUP CHOPPED ONION

2 GARLIC CLOVES, MINCED

½ CUP CHOPPED CARROT

¼ CUP CHOPPED CELERY

3 BONELESS, SKINLESS CHICKEN THIGHS, CUBED

2½ CUPS LOW-SODIUM CHICKEN BROTH

½ TEASPOON SALT

½ TEASPOON POULTRY SEASONING

⅓ CUP THIN EGG NOODLES

2 TABLESPOONS CHOPPED FRESH PARSLEY LEAVES

1. Combine the onion, garlic, carrot, celery, chicken, broth, salt, and poultry seasoning in the slow cooker. Cover and cook on low for 7 hours, or until the vegetables are tender and the chicken registers 160°F on an instant-read thermometer.

2. Stir in the noodles, cover, and cook for 10 to 15 minutes until al dente. Sprinkle the soup with parsley and serve immediately.

French Onion and Cabbage Soup

SERVES 2

Prep time: 15 minutes
Cook time: 7 hours

Adding cabbage to the classic French onion soup turns this recipe into a delicious, nutrient-packed meal. Cabbage is a cruciferous vegetable, which helps reduce the risk of cancer. It contains phytochemicals that act as antioxidants in your body, reducing inflammation and boosting the immune system.

1 TABLESPOON EXTRA-VIRGIN OLIVE OIL

1 TABLESPOON UNSALTED BUTTER

1 CUP CHOPPED ONION

2 GARLIC CLOVES, MINCED

1½ CUPS CHOPPED GREEN CABBAGE

2½ CUPS LOW-SODIUM BEEF BROTH

¼ TEASPOON SALT

⅛ TEASPOON FRESHLY GROUND WHITE PEPPER

2 SLICES FRENCH BREAD

½ CUP SHREDDED SWISS CHEESE

1 TABLESPOON GRATED PARMESAN CHEESE

1. In a small skillet over medium heat, heat the olive oil and butter. Add the onion; cook and stir until the onion just starts to brown, 6 to 7 minutes. Add the garlic and cook for 1 minute longer. Place the mixture in the slow cooker.

2. Add the cabbage, broth, salt, and white pepper. Cover and cook on low for 7 hours or until the vegetables are tender.

3. When you are ready to eat, heat a dry skillet over medium-high heat. Place the bread in the skillet and toast it for 1 to 2 minutes until golden brown. Turn the bread over and top with the cheeses. Toast the bread until the cheese is melted and starts to brown, 1 to 2 minutes longer.

4. Spoon the soup into two large bowls. Top with the bread and serve immediately.

Curried Chicken Soup

SERVES 2

Prep time: 15 minutes
Cook time: 6 hours

The flavor of curry, which is spicy and sweet, provides the perfect complement to tender chicken. And it doesn't hurt that curry powder is rich in essential nutrients. Did you know that turmeric, an ingredient in curry powder that adds the yellow color, blocks the formation of cancer cells in your body?

Curry powder is not an individual spice. It is a blend of many spices, including turmeric, coriander, ginger, mustard seed, cinnamon, cardamom, cumin, and peppers. In fact, in India many families have their own special blend of the spice mixture. Buy small quantities of different curry powder brands to find the one you like, or blend your own!

½ CUP CHOPPED ONION

1 GARLIC CLOVE, MINCED

2 BONELESS, SKINLESS CHICKEN BREASTS, CUBED

½ CUP FRESHLY SQUEEZED ORANGE JUICE

2 CUPS LOW-SODIUM CHICKEN BROTH

1 TO 2 TEASPOONS CURRY POWDER

½ CUP CHOPPED YELLOW BELL PEPPER

¼ CUP HEAVY CREAM

1 TABLESPOON CORNSTARCH

1. Combine the onion, garlic, chicken, juice, broth, and curry powder in the slow cooker. Cover and cook on low for 5 hours or until the vegetables are tender and the chicken registers 160°F on an instant-read thermometer.

2. Add the bell pepper to the slow cooker; cover and cook on low for 1 hour longer.

3. In a small bowl, whisk together the cream and cornstarch. Add the mixture to the slow cooker and stir well. Cover and cook on high for 10 to 15 minutes or until the soup thickens. Serve immediately.

Bean and Bacon Soup

Prep time: 20 minutes
Cook time: 8 hours

If the only bean and bacon soup you've tasted was from a can, you're in for a treat! This is an inexpensive recipe, and nothing is more hearty and comforting. Cooking the onion and garlic in some of the bacon fat before adding them to the slow cooker adds wonderful flavor.

¾ CUP NAVY BEANS, SORTED

3 SLICES BACON

½ CUP CHOPPED ONION

1 GARLIC CLOVE, MINCED

½ CUP CHOPPED CARROT

2½ CUPS WATER, PLUS MORE FOR COOKING THE BEANS

¼ TEASPOON DRIED THYME

¼ TEASPOON DRIED MARJORAM

1 TOMATO, CHOPPED

2 TABLESPOONS TOMATO PASTE

1 TABLESPOON MOLASSES

2 TABLESPOONS SOUR CREAM

2 TEASPOONS CORNSTARCH

1. In a medium saucepan, cover the beans with water. Bring the water to a boil, and let the beans cook in the boiling water for 2 minutes. Cover the pan, remove from the heat, and let stand for 1 hour. Drain the beans well and set aside.

2. In a small saucepan over medium heat, cook the bacon until crisp. Drain the bacon on paper towels, crumble, and set aside.

3. Add the onion and garlic to the bacon drippings remaining in the pan, and place the pan over medium heat. Cook for 4 to 5 minutes or until tender.

4. Combine onion-garlic mixture, beans, bacon, carrot, water, thyme, and marjoram in the slow cooker. Cover and cook on low for 6 to 7 hours or until the beans are tender.

5. Add the tomato and cook on high for 30 minutes.

6. In a small bowl, combine the tomato paste, molasses, sour cream, and cornstarch. Add ¼ cup of liquid from the slow cooker and mix well. Stir the mixture into the slow cooker. Cover and cook on high for 10 to 15 minutes longer, or until the soup is thickened. Serve hot.

Many Bean Soup

SERVES 2

Prep time: 5 minutes
Cook time: 8 hours

You can buy bean blends at the grocery store or you can combine different types of dried beans to make your own. The blends usually include pinto beans, great northern beans, lima beans, and dried split peas. The beans and legumes simmer to perfect tenderness in the slow cooker. You must start this recipe the day before because the beans have to soak overnight.

⅓ CUP DRIED PINTO BEANS

⅓ CUP DRIED GREAT NORTHERN BEANS

2 TABLESPOONS YELLOW SPLIT PEAS, RINSED

2 TABLESPOONS GREEN LENTILS, RINSED

3½ CUPS LOW-SODIUM VEGETABLE BROTH

½ CUP CHOPPED ONION

¼ CUP CHOPPED CELERY

1 GARLIC CLOVE, MINCED

¼ TEASPOON DRIED ITALIAN SEASONING

1 LARGE TOMATO, CHOPPED

1. Sort the beans and rinse; drain. Place them in a large bowl, cover them with water, and let them soak overnight.

2. In the morning, drain the beans. Combine the beans, split peas, and lentils in the slow cooker.

3. Add all remaining ingredients except for the tomato. Cover and cook on low for 7 hours, or until the beans are tender.

4. Stir in the tomato. Cover and cook on low for 1 hour longer, or until the flavors have melded. Serve hot.

Seafood Stew

Prep time: 15 minutes
Cook time: 7½ hours

The seafood stays tender in this easy recipe because it's added at the end of the cooking time. Most cubed fish fillets cook in about 15 minutes on low, and shellfish such as shrimp and mussels cook in about 5 to 10 minutes. You can use any type of seafood you like in this easy and delicious dish. Use a 1½-quart slow cooker for this recipe.

You must follow certain rules when cooking bivalve shellfish such as clams and mussels. First, the shellfish should be tightly closed before cooking. Discard any that are open and any that do not close when you tap the shells. And the shellfish should be open after cooking. Discard any that do not open. Mussels have hairy threads attached to their shells that help them cling to rocks. These hairy threads must be removed before cooking. Just pull them off and scrub the shells.

½ CUP CHOPPED ONION

1 CELERY STALK, CHOPPED

½ CUP PEELED, CHOPPED POTATO

2 GARLIC CLOVES, MINCED

3 TABLESPOONS TOMATO PASTE

1 CUP CLAM JUICE

⅓ CUP DRY WHITE WINE

2 CUPS WATER

½ TEASPOON OLD BAY SEASONING

¼ POUND RED SNAPPER, CUT INTO 1-INCH PIECES

⅓ POUND UNCOOKED MEDIUM SHRIMP, PEELED AND DEVEINED

½ POUND MUSSELS, SCRUBBED AND DEBEARDED

¼ CUP HEAVY CREAM

2 TABLESPOONS CHOPPED FRESH PARSLEY LEAVES

continued ▶

1. Combine the onion, celery, potato, garlic, tomato paste, clam juice, wine, water, and Old Bay seasoning in the slow cooker. Cover and cook on low for 7 hours.

2. Add the snapper to the slow cooker and stir gently. Cover and cook on low for 10 minutes. Add the shrimp and mussels; cover and cook on low for another 5 minutes.

3. Stir in the cream; cover and cook on low for 5 minutes or until the mussels open and soup is heated through. Sprinkle with parsley and serve immediately.

Minestrone Soup

Prep time: 20 minutes
Cook time: 8½ hours

Minestrone is simply a rich vegetable soup with pasta. The classic ingredients used in this recipe are onions, garlic, carrots, mushrooms, and celery, but feel free to add peas, green beans, zucchini, or any of your favorite vegetables. You could also add a can of drained cannellini beans for more volume.

2 CUPS LOW-SODIUM CHICKEN BROTH
¾ CUP TOMATO JUICE
¼ TEASPOON DRIED OREGANO
¼ CUP CHOPPED ONION
1 CELERY STALK, CHOPPED
½ CUP CHOPPED BUTTERNUT SQUASH
⅓ CUP CHOPPED TOMATO
¼ CUP CHOPPED GREEN BELL PEPPER
1 GARLIC CLOVE, MINCED
½ CUP CANNED RED KIDNEY BEANS, RINSED AND DRAINED
1 CUP CHOPPED SPINACH
½ CUP ORECCHIETTE OR MINI SHELL PASTA
GRATED PARMESAN CHEESE (OPTIONAL)
CHOPPED FLAT LEAF PARSLEY (OPTIONAL)

1. Combine all the ingredients except for the spinach, pasta, Parmesan cheese and parsley in the slow cooker.

2. Add the spinach and pasta and stir gently. Make sure the pasta is covered with the liquid. Cover and cook on high for 20 to 25 minutes longer until the pasta is tender. Serve with Parmesan cheese and parsley (if using).

Pasta e Fagioli

SERVES 2 TO 3

Prep time: 20 minutes
Cook time: 7½ hours

This classic Italian recipe is often called "pasta fazool". It is rich and hearty, made with beef, vegetables, beans, and pasta, "fasule" means beans in Neapolitan. The pasta cooks in the slow cooker with the other ingredients, so it picks up all of the rich flavors.

½ POUND GROUND BEEF

⅓ CUP CHOPPED ONION

1 GARLIC CLOVE, MINCED

1 SMALL CARROT, CHOPPED

1 CELERY STALK, CHOPPED

ONE 15-OUNCE CAN RED KIDNEY BEANS, DRAINED

ONE 14-OUNCE CAN DICED TOMATOES, UNDRAINED

1 CUP LOW-SODIUM BEEF BROTH

½ CUP PREPARED SPAGHETTI SAUCE

½ TEASPOON SALT

½ TEASPOON DRIED OREGANO

½ TEASPOON DRIED BASIL

FRESHLY GROUND BLACK PEPPER

½ CUP DITALINI PASTA

GRATED PARMESAN CHEESE (OPTIONAL)

1. In a medium skillet over medium heat, cook the ground beef with the onion and garlic for 5 to 6 minutes, stirring to break up the meat, until the beef is no longer pink. Drain well and place the mixture in the slow cooker.

2. Add the carrot, celery, kidney beans, tomatoes, broth, spaghetti sauce, salt, oregano, basil, and pepper to the slow cooker and stir. Cover and cook on low for 7 hours.

3. Add the pasta to the slow cooker. Cover and cook on low for 20 to 30 minutes or until the pasta is tender. Serve with grated Parmesan cheese (if using).

Corn and Sausage Chowder

SERVES 2 TO 3

Prep time: 20 minutes
Cook time: 6½ hours

Chowders are thicker than stews, and they are usually made with potatoes and some sort of dairy, such as cream or milk. This rich and thick recipe is very comforting and perfect for a cold winter day. Serve it with some toasted French bread slices spread with garlic butter.

½ POUND SWEET ITALIAN SAUSAGE, CASINGS REMOVED
½ CUP CHOPPED ONION
1 GARLIC CLOVE, MINCED
½ CUP DICED RED POTATOES
½ CUP FROZEN CORN KERNELS
ONE 8-OUNCE CAN CREAMED CORN
1½ CUPS LOW-SODIUM CHICKEN BROTH
¼ TEASPOON SALT
¼ TEASPOON DRIED THYME
½ CUP LIGHT CREAM
2 TEASPOONS CORNSTARCH

1. In a small skillet over medium heat, cook the sausage with the onion and garlic, stirring to break up the meat, until the sausage is no longer pink, about 5 minutes. Drain well.

2. Place the sausage mixture in the slow cooker along with the potatoes, corn kernels, creamed corn, chicken broth, salt, and thyme. Cover and cook on low for 6 hours.

3. In a small bowl, whisk together the cream and cornstarch, then stir it into the slow cooker. Cover and cook on low for 30 minutes or until the chowder thickens. Serve hot.

Loaded Baked Potato Chowder

SERVES 2

Prep time: 15 minutes
Cook time: 7 hours

When you think of baked potatoes, you probably think of bacon, green onions, and cheese—all ingredients in this fantastic soup! You can mash the potatoes right in the slow cooker; just use an immersion blender or a handheld potato masher.

3 SLICES BACON
½ CUP CHOPPED ONION
1 GARLIC CLOVE, MINCED
2 MEDIUM RUSSET POTATOES, PEELED AND CHOPPED
2 CUPS LOW-SODIUM CHICKEN BROTH
1 CUP WHOLE MILK
ONE 3-OUNCE PACKAGE CREAM CHEESE, AT ROOM TEMPERATURE
¼ CUP CHOPPED GREEN ONIONS, WHITE AND GREEN PARTS
1 CUP GRATED CHEDDAR CHEESE
1 TABLESPOON MINCED FRESH CHIVES

1. In a small skillet over medium heat, cook the bacon until crisp. Drain the bacon on paper towels, crumble, and set aside in the refrigerator. Add the onion and garlic to the bacon drippings remaining in the skillet and cook until the onions are translucent, about 5 minutes.

2. Place the onion-garlic mixture in the slow cooker along with the potatoes and broth. Cover and cook on low for 6 hours.

3. Using a potato masher or an immersion blender, mash the potatoes in the slow cooker. Then add the milk and cream cheese and mash again. Cover and cook on low for 30 minutes; stir well.

4. Add the bacon, green onions, and cheese. Cover and cook on low for 20 to 25 minutes or until the cheese is melted and the soup is hot. Sprinkle with chives and serve immediately.

Black Bean Chili

SERVES 2

Prep time: 15 minutes
Cook time: 8 hours

Black beans, also called turtle beans, have a black skin with a creamy white interior. They are tender but not mushy, and are delicious in chili. This vegetarian chili is a satisfying choice for those who are watching their fat intake. If you're not watching your fat intake, serve it with some sour cream and grated Cheddar cheese. You must start this recipe the day before because the beans have to soak overnight.

You can thicken any chili recipe if you like. Just combine 2 teaspoons of cornstarch with 2 tablespoons of water and mix well. Stir the mixture into the chili, cover, and cook for 15 to 20 minutes until it thickens. Alternately, you can mash some of the beans after they have softened. The starch in the beans will help to thicken the liquid.

1 CUP DRIED BLACK BEANS
½ CUP CHOPPED ONION
1 GARLIC CLOVE, MINCED
5 BUTTON MUSHROOMS, CHOPPED
2 TEASPOONS CHILI POWDER
2½ CUPS LOW-SODIUM VEGETABLE BROTH
½ CUP FROZEN CORN KERNELS
1 TOMATO, CHOPPED

1. Pick over the beans, rinse them, and drain. Cover the beans with cold water, cover, and let soak overnight. If you don't have time to let the beans soak overnight, place the beans in a saucepan and cover them with water. Bring the water to a boil over high heat and boil for 2 minutes. Cover the pan, remove it from the heat, and let stand for 1 hour. Drain the beans.

2. Combine the soaked beans, onion, garlic, mushrooms, chili powder, and broth in the slow cooker. Cover and cook on low for 7 hours or until the beans are tender. Add the corn and tomatoes and cook for 1 hour longer. Thicken the chili if you like with a cornstarch slurry (see tip).

White Chili

Prep time: 10 minutes
Cook time: 7½ hours

White chili is made with chicken, white beans, and green salsa. This rich and thick recipe is delicious topped with sour cream, chopped avocados, and minced cilantro. Chicken thighs are used because they stay tender even with this longer cooking time.

3 BONELESS, SKINLESS CHICKEN THIGHS, CUBED
½ CUP CHOPPED ONION
1 GARLIC CLOVE, MINCED
½ JALAPEÑO PEPPER, MINCED
ONE 15-OUNCE CAN CANNELLINI BEANS, RINSED AND DRAINED
2½ CUPS LOW-SODIUM CHICKEN BROTH
½ CUP GREEN SALSA (SALSA VERDE)
½ TEASPOON GROUND CUMIN
¼ TEASPOON DRIED OREGANO
¼ TEASPOON SALT
⅛ TEASPOON FRESHLY GROUND BLACK PEPPER
1 CUP SHREDDED PEPPER JACK CHEESE
2 TEASPOONS CORNSTARCH

1. Combine all ingredients except cheese and cornstarch in the slow cooker. Cover and cook on low for 7 hours, or until the chicken registers 160°F on an instant-read thermometer.

2. Toss the cheese with the cornstarch in a small bowl and add the mixture to the slow cooker; stir. Cover and cook on low for 15 to 20 minutes or until the cheese is melted and chili thickens. Serve hot.

Tex-Mex Chili

Prep time: 10 minutes
Cook time: 7 hours

Tex-Mex chili is rich and thick with beef and beans, spiced with several kinds of peppers. This easy recipe is delicious served with corn bread hot out of the oven. You can substitute spicy pork sausage for the beef if you'd like.

½ POUND GROUND BEEF
½ CUP CHOPPED ONION
2 GARLIC CLOVES, MINCED
1 SMALL JALAPEÑO PEPPER, MINCED
ONE 15-OUNCE CAN RED KIDNEY BEANS, RINSED AND DRAINED
2 TEASPOONS CHILI POWDER
½ TEASPOON GROUND CUMIN
¼ TEASPOON SALT
⅛ TEASPOON RED PEPPER FLAKES
1½ CUPS LOW-SODIUM BEEF BROTH
1 CUP SALSA
GRATED CHEDDAR CHEESE, GUACAMOLE, AND SOUR CREAM (OPTIONAL)

1. In a small skillet over medium heat, cook the ground beef with the onion and garlic, stirring to break up the meat, until browned, about 5 minutes. Drain well.

2. Add the ground beef mixture to the slow cooker, along with the jalapeño, beans, chili powder, cumin, salt, red pepper flakes, broth, and salsa. Cover and cook on low for 7 hours until blended.

3. Serve with grated Cheddar cheese, guacamole, and sour cream (if using).

Wild Rice Chili

Prep time: 15 minutes
Cook time: 8 hours

Wild rice is a fabulous addition to chili. The nutty taste and tender texture complement the beans and meatless crumbles in this easy recipe. Always buy wild rice with the longest grains possible. Broken wild rice, which is less expensive, will almost always become mushy when cooked. Use a 2-quart slow cooker for this recipe.

⅓ CUP WILD RICE, RINSED

½ CUP CHOPPED ONION

1 GARLIC CLOVE, MINCED

1 CUP FROZEN MEATLESS CRUMBLES (FROM A 16-OUNCE BAG)

ONE 14-OUNCE CAN DICED TOMATOES, UNDRAINED

ONE 15-OUNCE CAN BLACK BEANS, RINSED AND DRAINED

2½ CUPS LOW-SODIUM VEGETABLE BROTH

2 TEASPOONS CHILI POWDER

¼ TEASPOON SALT

⅛ TEASPOON FRESHLY GROUND BLACK PEPPER

1. Combine all the ingredients in the slow cooker.

2. Cover and cook on low for 7 to 8 hours or until the wild rice is tender. Serve hot.

CHAPTER SIX

Vegetarian Sides and Entrées

You might not think of the slow cooker as a vegetarian's dream but, in fact, it is an ideal vessel for cooking just about any kind of vegetable. With very little oil required, slow cookers can wilt fresh greens, steam tender asparagus spears, and roast potatoes and other root vegetables to caramelized perfection. They are also great for risottos, curries, and casseroles of all kinds.

For vegetarian side dishes, the slow cooker is indispensable, freeing up your stove top and oven for other components of the meal while trapping the rich nutrients and flavor that pan-frying or oven-roasting might let escape. And for vegetarian entrées, slow cookers provide a forgiving method for experimenting with non-meat proteins and sources of other essential amino acids.

In order for a vegetarian recipe to be called an entrée, it must contain protein, which can be provided by the inclusion of dairy products, eggs, or complete proteins formed by combinations of grains, legumes, seeds, or nuts. Vegetarian entrées that do not contain any dairy products or eggs are considered vegan.

Whether you are looking for a vegetarian entrée or a side to accompany one of the other main course recipes in this book, you will be amazed by the slow cooker's versatility. Use these recipes as guidelines to create your own masterpieces. For instance, use different vegetables in the Vegetable Couscous Stuffed Peppers. Use different cheeses in the Mac and Cheese. Add your favorite vegetables to the Barley Risotto. And above all else, have fun experimenting with your partner in the kitchen!

ROASTED VEGETABLES

STEAMED ARTICHOKES

ROASTED NEW POTATOES

SLOW COOKER MASHED POTATOES

MAC AND CHEESE

RAVIOLI LASAGNA

CREAMY PARMESAN RISOTTO

BARLEY RISOTTO

CAULIFLOWER CURRY

VEGETABLE COUSCOUS STUFFED PEPPERS

Roasted Vegetables

SERVES 2

Prep time: 15 minutes
Cook time: 6 hours

All of these vegetables roast for the same amount of time, even though the recipe mixes hard and soft produce. That means the bell pepper and yellow squash will become very tender and sweet, while the sweet potato will be tender, but a bit firmer. You could substitute green beans, baby carrots, or corn if you'd like. Try your favorite dried herbs in this easy dish.

1 RED BELL PEPPER, THICKLY SLICED

½ CUP SLICED RED ONION

1 SMALL YELLOW SQUASH, THICKLY SLICED

2 GARLIC CLOVES, SLICED

1 MEDIUM SWEET POTATO, PEELED AND CUT INTO ½-INCH CUBES

½ TEASPOON SALT

⅛ TEASPOON FRESHLY GROUND BLACK PEPPER

1 TEASPOON DRIED ITALIAN SEASONING

2 TABLESPOONS EXTRA-VIRGIN OLIVE OIL

1. Combine all the ingredients in the slow cooker.

2. Cover and cook on low until all of the vegetables are tender, about 6 hours, stirring once during the cooking time.

Steamed Artichokes

Prep time: 20 minutes
Cook time: 6 hours

Artichokes look like they're difficult to prepare and cook, but they're not. You just need to know a few tricks. Cut off the bottom stem, and then cut off the top inch. Pull off the outer layer of leaves and trim the sharp tip off the remaining leaves with a pair of kitchen shears. If you like, you can open the artichoke to remove the choke, which is the part that looks like a thistle, but you don't have to. Artichokes turn brown easily, so rub the cut edges with lemon. Then cook them and enjoy!

2 TO 3 LARGE ARTICHOKES
1 TABLESPOON FRESHLY SQUEEZED LEMON JUICE
1 CUP WATER
2 LEMON SLICES
MELTED BUTTER, FOR DIPPING

1. Prepare the artichokes according to the instructions in the headnote, and place them in the slow cooker, stem-side down.

2. In a small bowl, combine the lemon juice and water and pour the mixture over and around the artichokes. Top each artichoke with a lemon slice.

3. Cover and cook on low for 5 to 6 hours or until a leaf pulls out easily from each artichoke.

4. To eat, pull off each leaf, dip it in butter, and scrape the tender end between your teeth to remove the flesh. When all the leaves are off, remove the choke if it wasn't removed previously, cut the artichoke heart (the area above the stem) into pieces and eat.

Roasted New Potatoes

Prep time: 15 minutes
Cook time: 4 hours

These potatoes are tender and flavorful. Use your favorite herbs in this easy recipe. New potatoes are small, about 1 to 2 inches in diameter, usually with tender red skins. All you need to do before cooking them is to scrub the skins gently and cut them in half or into quarters, depending on their size. This is an excellent side dish to serve with grilled chicken or steak.

1 POUND SMALL NEW RED POTATOES

2 GARLIC CLOVES, SLICED

1 TABLESPOON EXTRA-VIRGIN OLIVE OIL

2 TABLESPOONS UNSALTED BUTTER, MELTED

2 TEASPOONS CHOPPED FRESH THYME LEAVES

1 TEASPOON CHOPPED FRESH OREGANO LEAVES

¼ TEASPOON SALT

1. Cut the potatoes into halves or quarters, depending on the size, to make about 1-inch pieces.

2. Combine all of the ingredients in the slow cooker. Cover and cook on high for 3 to 4 hours or until the potatoes are tender when pierced with a knife.

Slow Cooker Mashed Potatoes

Prep time: 15 minutes
Cook time: 5 hours

Mashed potatoes are always a favorite, and they cook so well in the slow cooker. Russet potatoes are really best for making mashed potatoes because they are mealy, which creates the best texture. You can keep these potatoes warm in the slow cooker for up to two hours after you have mashed them.

1 POUND RUSSET POTATOES, PEELED AND CUT INTO 1-INCH CHUNKS
1 CUP WATER
ONE 3-OUNCE PACKAGE CREAM CHEESE, AT ROOM TEMPERATURE
⅓ CUP SOUR CREAM
3 TABLESPOONS WHOLE MILK
1 TABLESPOON UNSALTED BUTTER
¼ TEASPOON SALT
⅛ TEASPOON FRESHLY GROUND BLACK PEPPER

1. Combine the potatoes and water in the slow cooker. Cover and cook on high for 4 hours or on low for 8 hours, until the potatoes are very tender.

2. Drain the potatoes well and return them to the warm slow cooker. Turn the slow cooker to low.

3. In a small microwave-safe bowl, combine the cream cheese, sour cream, milk, butter, salt, and pepper. Microwave the mixture on high power for 1 minute; remove the bowl from the microwave and stir the mixture with a wire whisk until it is combined.

4. Add the cream cheese mixture to the potatoes in the slow cooker and mash with a fork or a potato masher. Add more milk if needed for your desired consistency.

5. Cover and cook on low for 1 hour. Then turn the slow cooker to warm until ready to serve.

Mac and Cheese

Prep time: 10 minutes
Cook time: 4 hours

Macaroni and cheese is the ultimate comfort food, perfect for a cold winter night. The key to this recipe is to partially cook the macaroni in boiling water before you add it to the other ingredients, so it cooks through without becoming mushy. Evaporated milk is key to this recipe, too, since regular milk would curdle after long exposure to heat.

1½ CUPS DRY MACARONI NOODLES
ONE 5-OUNCE CAN EVAPORATED MILK
1½ CUPS WHOLE MILK
½ TEASPOON SALT
1 CUP SHREDDED SHARP CHEDDAR CHEESE
½ CUP SHREDDED MONTEREY JACK CHEESE
3 TABLESPOONS SOUR CREAM
2 TABLESPOONS UNSALTED BUTTER, MELTED

1. Bring a large pot of water to a boil. Cook the macaroni noodles for half the recommended cooking time. Drain well and add the noodles to the slow cooker.

2. Add all remaining ingredients to the slow cooker and stir well.

3. Cover and cook on low for 3 to 4 hours, stirring once about halfway through the cooking time, until the macaroni is tender and the cheese is melted. Serve hot.

Ravioli Lasagna

SERVES 2

Prep time: 20 minutes
Cook time: 6 hours

This super-simple recipe really does taste like lasagna, but you don't have to boil noodles or worry about layering four or five different mixtures. There are many flavors and varieties of frozen ravioli. Choose your favorite for this recipe. And don't thaw the ravioli before you add it to the slow cooker.

1 TABLESPOON UNSALTED BUTTER
½ CUP CHOPPED ONION
1 GARLIC CLOVE, MINCED
1⅔ CUPS SPAGHETTI SAUCE
2½ CUPS (ABOUT 10 OUNCES) FROZEN CHEESE RAVIOLI
½ CUP SOUR CREAM
1 CUP SHREDDED ITALIAN CHEESE BLEND
2 TABLESPOONS GRATED PARMESAN CHEESE

1. In a medium microwave-safe bowl, combine the butter, onion, and garlic. Microwave the mixture, uncovered, on high power for 2 minutes. Remove the bowl and stir in the spaghetti sauce.

2. Spoon ½ cup of the sauce mixture into the slow cooker. Top with half of the ravioli, half of the sour cream, and half of the Italian cheese blend. Repeat the layers, then sprinkle the top with Parmesan cheese.

3. Cover and cook on low for 5 to 6 hours or until the ravioli is tender. Serve hot.

Creamy Parmesan Risotto

SERVES 2

Prep time: 10 minutes
Cook time: 2½ hours

Risotto is something special. It's made of short-grain rice cooked in broth, finished with Parmesan cheese and butter. This creamy, velvety smooth, and rich recipe is delicious served with a simple green salad and some toasted garlic bread. You do need to use arborio rice in this recipe; it won't work as well with long-grain rice.

Arborio rice comes from Italy. It is the classic variety used to make risotto. Because it is a short-grain rice, it has more highly branched starch molecules, called amylopectin, than long-grain rice. That starch comes out of the rice while it cooks and makes the liquid very creamy, resulting in a velvety smooth texture without the addition of any cream.

1 CUP ARBORIO RICE

3 CUPS LOW-SODIUM VEGETABLE BROTH

3 TABLESPOONS DRY WHITE WINE

1 SMALL SHALLOT, MINCED

2 GARLIC CLOVES, MINCED

½ TEASPOON SALT

FRESHLY GROUND BLACK PEPPER

½ CUP GRATED PARMESAN CHEESE

2 TABLESPOONS UNSALTED BUTTER

1. Combine the rice, broth, wine, shallot, garlic, salt, and pepper in the slow cooker. Cover and cook on high for 2 hours, stirring once halfway through the cooking time.

2. Add the cheese and butter to the rice mixture. Cover and cook on low for 20 minutes, then stir.

3. Cover and cook on low for another 10 minutes or until the rice is tender and the mixture is creamy and hot. Serve immediately.

Barley Risotto

Prep time: 5 minutes
Cook time: 4½ hours

Barley makes an excellent risotto because the grains emit starch as they cook. Unlike a classic risotto, this recipe doesn't need any stirring at all. Barley is a whole grain that is high in fiber, which can help reduce the risk of high cholesterol. It also contains copper and phosphorous, some of the micronutrients you need for good health. Plus, it's nutty and delicious!

Leeks are members of the onion family. They look like large spring onions, and they have a milder taste than regular yellow onions. Leeks must be cleaned well before use. Wash the leeks and pull off the tough outside leaves. Cut off the root. Then cut the leek, starting at the white part, into rings; use just the bottom 3 inches of the green part. Immerse the rings in cool water, manipulating the leeks with your fingers, so the sand comes out of them. Carefully scoop the leeks out of the water, leaving the sand behind, and chop.

3 TABLESPOONS UNSALTED BUTTER
½ CUP MINCED LEEK, WHITE PART ONLY
6 BUTTON MUSHROOMS, SLICED
1¼ CUP PEARL BARLEY
½ TEASPOON DRIED THYME
2¾ CUPS LOW-SODIUM VEGETABLE BROTH
¼ CUP GRATED PARMESAN CHEESE

1. In a small saucepan, melt 1 tablespoon of the butter over medium heat. Add the leek and cook, stirring frequently, for 5 to 6 minutes until soft. Add the mushrooms; cook and stir for 1 minute longer.

2. Add the leek-mushroom mixture to the slow cooker, along with the barley, thyme, and broth. Stir to combine. Cover and cook on low for 4 hours or until the barley is tender.

3. Stir in the cheese and the remaining 2 tablespoons of butter. Cover and cook on low for 30 minutes. Stir again and serve.

Cauliflower Curry

Prep time: 20 minutes
Cook time: 5 hours

When purchasing cauliflower, look for white heads with tightly closed florets. There should be no or very few dark or brown spots on the head. Rinse the cauliflower and cut off the leaves and the large stem. Cut the florets into individual pieces about the same size so they cook evenly. Serve this recipe over hot cooked brown rice.

Curry paste is usually used in Thai cooking, while curry powder is used in Indian recipes. The two are not really interchangeable, since the paste can contain ginger, garlic, and other ingredients that make the mixture wet. Curry paste is usually stronger than curry powder. Red curry paste is the hottest, green is next hottest, and the yellow paste is more mild.

½ HEAD CAULIFLOWER, CUT INTO 1-INCH PIECES
1 SMALL RUSSET POTATO, PEELED AND DICED
½ CUP ONION, FINELY CHOPPED
1 GARLIC CLOVE, MINCED
1 TOMATO, CHOPPED
2 TEASPOONS YELLOW CURRY PASTE
¼ TEASPOON SALT
⅛ TEASPOON FRESHLY GROUND WHITE PEPPER
1 CUP LOW-SODIUM VEGETABLE BROTH
½ CUP COCONUT MILK

1. Combine all of the ingredients in the slow cooker.

2. Cover and cook on low for 4 to 5 hours or until the vegetables are tender.

Vegetable Couscous Stuffed Peppers

SERVES 2

Prep time: 20 minutes

Cook time: 7 hours

Peppers are wonderful containers for all types of stuffing. Use relatively large peppers so there's a lot of room for the delicious filling. The couscous must be rehydrated ahead of time in this recipe, because otherwise it would expand in the peppers and break them open.

½ CUP COUSCOUS

1 CUP LOW-SODIUM VEGETABLE BROTH, HEATED, PLUS ½ CUP UNHEATED

2 OR 3 RED OR GREEN BELL PEPPERS

½ CUP MINCED ONION

1 GARLIC CLOVE, MINCED

1 CUP FROZEN CORN KERNELS, THAWED

½ TEASPOON DRIED MARJORAM

½ TEASPOON SALT

⅛ TEASPOON FRESHLY GROUND BLACK PEPPER

1 CUP SHREDDED HAVARTI CHEESE

ONE 8-OUNCE CAN TOMATO SAUCE

3 TABLESPOONS GRATED PARMESAN CHEESE

1. In a small bowl, combine the couscous and 1 cup of hot broth. Cover and let stand for 5 minutes, then fluff with a fork.

2. Cut the tops off the bell peppers and carefully remove the membranes and seeds. Set aside.

3. In a medium bowl, combine the couscous, onion, garlic, corn, marjoram, salt, pepper, and Havarti cheese; mix well. Add 3 tablespoons of the tomato sauce. Stuff the mixture into the peppers and top with the Parmesan cheese.

4. Place the stuffed peppers in the slow cooker, stuffing-side up. In a small bowl, combine the remaining tomato sauce and the remaining ½ cup of vegetable broth. Pour the mixture around the peppers.

5. Cover and cook on low for 6 to 7 hours, or until the peppers are tender.

CHAPTER SEVEN

Fish and Seafood

From the classic American Tuna Noodle Casserole to fish prepared with flavors from South America, these fish and seafood dishes are as healthful as they are delicious. Fish is very low in fat and rich in protein, calcium, omega-3 fatty acids, vitamins such as B2 and D, and essential minerals such as iron, zinc, magnesium, and potassium that can lower blood pressure and help reduce the risk of stroke and heart attack.

So although cooking fish and seafood in a slow cooker takes a bit of maneuvering and timing, it's well worth it. Fish and seafood are delicate and can overcook easily. So to cook these foods in the slow cooker, just add them toward the end of the cooking time.

Fish should be cooked to 140°F. To test for doneness, insert a fork into the fish and twist gently. The fish will break apart. If it resists, cover the slow cooker and cook for an additional five to ten minutes. Shrimp will curl and turn pink when they are cooked. Mussels and clams will open when they are cooked to a safe temperature.

You can substitute other fish for the kinds called for in these recipes. Fish fillets to use include red snapper, cod, trout, tilapia, and mackerel.

Many of these recipes start with a flavor base or by cooking other foods, such as potatoes or carrots, until they are almost done. The seafood is then placed on top of the food already in the appliance. The fish will steam to perfection in the heat already built up in the slow cooker.

TUNA NOODLE CASSEROLE

SALMON PACKETS

ROASTED SALMON AND POTATOES

SHRIMP MARINARA

JAMBALAYA

LAYERED SEAFOOD TORTA

RED SNAPPER VERACRUZ

Tuna Noodle Casserole

SERVES 2

Prep time: 15 minutes
Cook time: 6 hours

The pasta cooks right in the liquid in this wonderful, comforting recipe, absorbing the rich flavors of the sauce. When you're buying tuna, make sure you look for the "dolphin safe" label. Chunk light tuna is the best type to use in this recipe. You can use a different type of cheese or add other veggies to this dish if you'd like.

1 CUP UNCOOKED EGG NOODLES

½ CUP FINELY CHOPPED ONION

½ CUP CHOPPED CELERY

1 GARLIC CLOVE, MINCED

1 CUP PREPARED ALFREDO SAUCE (FROM A 16-OUNCE JAR)

1 CUP WATER

½ CUP WHOLE MILK

ONE 6-OUNCE CAN CHUNK LIGHT TUNA, DRAINED

½ TEASPOON CELERY SEED

⅛ TEASPOON FRESHLY GROUND BLACK PEPPER

1 CUP SHREDDED HAVARTI CHEESE

½ CUP FROZEN PEAS

½ CUP CRUMBLED CRISP POTATO CHIPS

1. Combine the noodles, onion, celery, garlic, Alfredo sauce, water, and milk in the slow cooker and stir to combine. Add the tuna, celery seed, and pepper.

2. Cover and cook on low for 5 hours, stirring after the second and fourth hours.

3. Add the cheese and peas and stir gently. Cover and cook on low for 1 hour longer or until the noodles are tender and the cheese is melted.

4. Top each serving with the crumbled potato chips.

Salmon Packets

Prep time: 10 minutes
Cook time: 3 hours

For this recipe, you make two foil packets filled with salmon and vegetables. Seal the packets using a double fold, but allow room for expansion in the packet. Just place the packets side by side in the slow cooker and cook until the fish flakes. The fish will be very moist, tender, and well flavored.

- -

You can use this foil cooking method for other types of fish, too. Substitute fish fillets such as snapper or cod for the salmon. Foil packet cooking will also work with boneless, skinless chicken breasts and thighs. Just increase the cooking time. Other types of fish will cook in about the same time as the salmon, but chicken usually needs 5 to 7 hours in the slow cooker. Make sure you match the cooking time of the vegetables to the meat.

- -

4 LEMON SLICES
TWO 6-OUNCE SALMON FILLETS
⅛ TEASPOON SALT
FRESHLY GROUND BLACK PEPPER
½ TEASPOON DRIED MARJORAM
2 TABLESPOONS UNSALTED BUTTER, MELTED
1 CUP FROZEN GREEN BEANS, THAWED
¼ CUP CHOPPED GREEN ONION

1. Tear off two pieces of foil about 18 inches long and place them on a work surface. Arrange 2 lemon slices in the center of each piece, then top them with the salmon fillets.

2. Sprinkle with salt, pepper, and marjoram and drizzle with melted butter. Divide the beans and green onion between the two packets.

3. Bring the edges of the foil together over the food and seal it, using a double seal. Fold up the other ends to seal. Place the packets in the slow cooker, seam-side up.

4. Cover and cook on low for 2 to 3 hours or until the salmon flakes when tested with a fork. Unwrap the packets carefully, since the steam in the packets will be hot, and serve immediately.

Roasted Salmon and Potatoes

SERVES 2

Prep time: 15 minutes
Cook time: 7½ hours

The potatoes and leeks roast to tender perfection in this elegant recipe, and then the seasoned salmon is placed on top and steamed. This is a wonderful recipe for a special occasion. You can double it and serve it to company.

1 TABLESPOON EXTRA-VIRGIN OLIVE OIL

1 TABLESPOON UNSALTED BUTTER

½ CUP CHOPPED LEEKS, WHITE PART ONLY

2 GARLIC CLOVES, MINCED

2 RUSSET POTATOES, SCRUBBED AND CUT INTO 1-INCH CHUNKS

TWO 6-OUNCE SALMON FILLETS

¼ TEASPOON SALT

½ TEASPOON DRIED THYME

⅛ TEASPOON FRESHLY GROUND BLACK PEPPER

1. Combine the olive oil, butter, leeks, garlic, and potatoes in the slow cooker. Cover and cook on low for 6 to 7 hours or until the vegetables are almost tender. Stir gently.

2. Sprinkle the salmon fillets with salt, thyme, and pepper and place them on top of the potatoes. Cover and cook on low for 30 to 40 minutes or until the salmon flakes when tested with a fork. Serve hot.

Shrimp Marinara

Prep time: 15 minutes

Cook time: 4 hours

Marinara is simply a tomato sauce, usually flavored with oregano and basil and cooked with garlic and onion. It's a delicious foil for tender shrimp. The sauce cooks first, and then you add the uncooked shrimp. Serve over hot cooked rice or spaghetti.

ONE 14-OUNCE CAN DICED TOMATOES, UNDRAINED

2 TABLESPOONS TOMATO PASTE

½ CUP LOW-SODIUM CHICKEN BROTH

½ CUP DICED ONION

2 GARLIC CLOVES, MINCED

½ TEASPOON DRIED ITALIAN SEASONING

¾ POUND UNCOOKED MEDIUM SHRIMP, PEELED AND DEVEINED

1. Combine all the ingredients except the shrimp in the slow cooker. Cover and cook on low for 4 hours.

2. Add the shrimp and stir. Cover and cook on low for 10 to 15 minutes longer, just until the shrimp curl and turn pink. Serve over spaghetti.

Jambalaya

SERVES 2

Prep time: 20 minutes
Cook time: 7½ hours

Jambalaya is a delicious casserole featuring sausage and shrimp. The sausage needs to be browned before it's added to the vegetables, and the shrimp is added at the end of the cooking time. Serve this recipe in big bowls with some extra hot sauce on the side if you like it spicy.

Most shrimp is sold with the shells on. To remove the shell, peel it off, starting with the head. You can leave the tail on or pull it off, depending on your taste. Then cut a very thin slit along the back of the shrimp where you see a dark line; this is the vein. Pull out the vein and rinse the peeled shrimp. The shrimp is ready to use!

2 LINKS PORK SAUSAGE
½ CUP CHOPPED ONION
1 GARLIC CLOVE, MINCED
1 CELERY STALK, CHOPPED
¼ CUP CHOPPED GREEN BELL PEPPER
½ TEASPOON CAJUN SEASONING BLEND
ONE 14-OUNCE CAN DICED TOMATOES, UNDRAINED
1 CUP LOW-SODIUM CHICKEN BROTH
½ POUND UNCOOKED MEDIUM SHRIMP, PEELED AND DEVEINED
1 TO 2 DROPS HOT SAUCE
½ CUP INSTANT RICE
2 TABLESPOONS CHOPPED FLAT-LEAF PARSLEY LEAVES

1. Cut the pork sausage into ½-inch pieces. In a small saucepan over medium heat, cook the sausage with the onion and garlic, stirring frequently, until sausage is browned, about 5 minutes.

2. Place the sausage mixture, celery, bell pepper, Cajun seasoning, tomatoes, and broth in the slow cooker. Cover and cook on low for 6 to 7 hours until the vegetables are tender and the flavors have melded.

3. Add the shrimp and hot sauce to the slow cooker. Cover and cook on low for 10 to 15 minutes or until the shrimp curl and turn pink. Add the rice; turn off the heat and let it stand for 10 minutes. Stir, sprinkle with parsley, and serve immediately.

Layered Seafood Torta

Prep time: 15 minutes
Cook time: 5 hours

The seafood in this recipe is fully cooked before you layer it in the slow cooker and turn it on. The slow cooker simply heats all of the ingredients so the flavors blend and the cheese melts. Serve this torta with a green salad tossed with sliced mushrooms and avocado, along with some fresh fruit such as melon or grapes.

1 TABLESPOON UNSALTED BUTTER
½ CUP CHOPPED ONION
2 GARLIC CLOVES, MINCED
1 TEASPOON CHILI POWDER
¼ TEASPOON GROUND CUMIN
½ TEASPOON DRIED OREGANO
1 CUP FROZEN CORN KERNELS, THAWED AND DRAINED
½ CUP PREPARED ALFREDO SAUCE (FROM A 16-OUNCE JAR)
½ CUP SOUR CREAM
1 CUP SHREDDED MONTEREY JACK CHEESE
1½ CUPS (ABOUT ¾ POUND) SMALL COOKED SHRIMP
ONE 6-OUNCE CAN CRABMEAT, DRAINED
COOKING SPRAY
THREE 8-INCH FLOUR TORTILLAS
3 TABLESPOONS GRATED PARMESAN CHEESE

1. In a small skillet over medium heat, melt the butter. Add the onion and garlic; cook and stir until tender, 4 to 5 minutes. Add the chili powder, cumin, oregano, and corn and remove the pan from the heat. Stir in the Alfredo sauce, sour cream, and Monterey Jack cheese.

2. In a small bowl, combine the shrimp and crabmeat.

3. Spray the slow cooker with cooking spray. Place about ½ cup of the sauce mixture in the bottom. Top with 1 tortilla, then half of the seafood mixture, then half of the sauce mixture. Repeat the layers, ending with a tortilla. Top with the Parmesan cheese.

4. Cover the slow cooker and cook on low for 4 to 5 hours, or until the torta is heated through and the cheese has melted.

5. Cut the torta into wedges and serve immediately.

Red Snapper Veracruz

Prep time: 15 minutes
Cook time: 7½ hours

Veracruz is a Mexican port town on the Gulf of Mexico. It has wonderful seafood in the waters off the coast, and delicious recipes to cook it. This sauce is rich with onion, garlic, cinnamon, tomatoes, olives, and capers. Use red snapper if you can find it, but cod and other white fish fillets will work well, too.

½ CUP CHOPPED ONION
1 GARLIC CLOVE, MINCED
½ JALAPEÑO PEPPER, MINCED
¼ TEASPOON DRIED OREGANO
⅛ TEASPOON GROUND CINNAMON
2 LARGE TOMATOES, DICED
1 TABLESPOON CAPERS
¼ CUP SLICED STUFFED GREEN OLIVES
½ CUP TOMATO JUICE
1 TABLESPOON FRESHLY SQUEEZED LEMON JUICE
TWO 6-OUNCE RED SNAPPER FILLETS

1. Combine all the ingredients except the lemon juice and snapper in the slow cooker. Cover and cook on low for 6 to 7 hours.

2. Stir in the lemon juice, and then place the snapper in the slow cooker. Cover and cook on high for 15 to 20 minutes or until the fish flakes when tested with a fork. Serve immediately.

CHAPTER EIGHT

Poultry

Boneless, skinless chicken breasts and thighs are delicious and easy to use in many different slow cooker recipes. They also work better in slow cookers than skin-on chicken breasts and thighs because the skin tends to turn mushy or rubbery when cooked this way. Skinless chicken thighs are preferable for longer-cooking recipes, since they have more fat to keep them moist, but chicken breasts work well in the slow cooker as long as they are not overcooked.

Old recipes for chicken breasts that cook for eight or nine hours usually overcook with the hotter, newer appliances. If you have a newer model (made later than the 1990s), reduce the cooking time in those older recipes to about five to six hours. If you're not sure whether you have a "new" or "old" slow cooker, watch your chicken or meat closely and take note of when it reaches the desired internal temperature for doneness, then adjust all future recipes accordingly. Always cook chicken to 160°F as tested with an instant-read thermometer.

Chicken combines well with ingredients from every cuisine around the world. These recipes show you the range of ideas, from a comforting and classic Chicken and Dumplings to Coq au Vin from France, Butter Chicken from India, and Chicken Mole from Mexico.

CHICKEN PARMESAN

CHICKEN AND DUMPLINGS

CHICKEN POT PIE

CREAMY CHICKEN WITH PENNE

COQ AU VIN

GREEK CHICKEN SANDWICHES

BUTTER CHICKEN

LASAGNA CHICKEN ROLLUPS

CHICKEN CACCIATORE

STICKY CHICKEN

CHICKEN ENCHILADAS

CHICKEN MOLE

Chicken Parmesan

Prep time: 5 minutes
Cook time: 5 hours

Regular chicken Parmesan is coated with bread crumbs, sautéed, then cooked in a marinara sauce and served over cooked spaghetti. In a slow cooker, the bread crumbs are sprinkled on top of the dish just before serving, so they don't get mushy. This flavorful entrée is a wonderful way to use chicken breasts.

2 BONELESS, SKINLESS CHICKEN BREASTS
½ TEASPOON DRIED ITALIAN SEASONING
½ TEASPOON SALT
⅛ TEASPOON FRESHLY GROUND BLACK PEPPER
1½ CUPS SPAGHETTI SAUCE
½ CUP MINCED ONION
1 GARLIC CLOVE, MINCED
1 TABLESPOON UNSALTED BUTTER
5 TABLESPOONS PANKO BREAD CRUMBS
HOT COOKED SPAGHETTI
GRATED PARMESAN CHEESE (OPTIONAL)

1. Sprinkle the chicken breasts with Italian seasoning, salt, and pepper.

2. In a slow cooker, combine the spaghetti sauce, onion, and garlic. Top the mixture with the chicken.

3. Cover and cook on low for 5 hours, or until the chicken registers 160°F on an instant-read thermometer.

4. When the chicken is almost done, melt the butter in a small saucepan over medium heat. Sauté the bread crumbs until golden brown.

5. Serve the chicken and sauce over hot cooked spaghetti; sprinkle with bread crumbs and Parmesan cheese (if using).

Chicken and Dumplings

Prep time: 15 minutes
Cook time: 5½ hours

Dumplings are like biscuits, but instead of being baked in the oven, they are simmered in broth on top of the stove. They cook well in the slow cooker. There are a few rules about making the best dumplings. First, stir only until the batter comes together. If you beat the batter, the dumplings will be tough. Second, drop the dumplings into simmering broth. And third, don't lift the lid while the dumplings are cooking.

. . . .

Chicken cooked on the bone is more flavorful than boneless chicken, and it takes longer to cook. You can use bone-in chicken in any recipe if you'd like; just add another hour or two to the cooking time. To remove chicken skin, just use a paper towel (because the skin is slippery) and firmly pull it off. You may have to cut off any remaining stubborn pieces. Discard the skin.

. . . .

2 BONE-IN CHICKEN BREASTS, SKIN REMOVED

1 CUP PLUS 2 TABLESPOONS ALL-PURPOSE FLOUR

¾ TEASPOON SALT

⅛ TEASPOON FRESHLY GROUND BLACK PEPPER

½ TEASPOON DRIED MARJORAM

1 SMALL POTATO, CHOPPED

½ CUP CHOPPED ONION

2 GARLIC CLOVES, MINCED

1 SMALL CARROT, PEELED AND SLICED

1 CELERY STALK, SLICED

1¼ CUPS LOW-SODIUM CHICKEN BROTH

½ CUP FROZEN BABY PEAS

½ TEASPOON BAKING POWDER

2 TABLESPOONS UNSALTED BUTTER

¼ CUP WHOLE MILK

continued ▶

1. Sprinkle the chicken with 2 tablespoons flour, ½ teaspoon salt, black pepper, and marjoram leaves and set aside.

2. Combine the potato, onion, garlic, carrot, and celery in slow cooker. Place the chicken on top of the vegetables. Pour in 1 cup of the broth.

3. Cover and cook on low for 5 hours. Add the peas, stir, and turn the heat to high.

4. In a small bowl, combine the remaining 1 cup of flour, baking powder, and remaining ¼ teaspoon salt. Cut the butter into the flour mixture in small pieces. Add the remaining ¼ cup broth and milk, and stir just until the dough forms.

5. Drop the dumplings by the tablespoonful into the slow cooker. Cover and cook on high for 20 to 30 minutes or until a toothpick inserted into the dumplings comes out clean. Serve immediately.

Chicken Pot Pie

Prep time: 15 minutes
Cook time: 9 hours

Pie crust doesn't cook well in a slow cooker. So cook one in the oven, and top each serving with a crisp wedge. This comforting and easy recipe is perfect for a cold night. The house will smell amazing when you get home!

4 BONELESS, SKINLESS CHICKEN THIGHS, CUBED
½ CUP MINCED ONION
2 GARLIC CLOVES, MINCED
1 CELERY STALK, CHOPPED
1 CUP BABY CARROTS
1 CUP PREPARED ALFREDO SAUCE (FROM A 16-OUNCE JAR)
½ TEASPOON POULTRY SEASONING
1 CUP FROZEN BABY PEAS
1 REFRIGERATED PIE CRUST
2 TABLESPOONS GRATED PARMESAN CHEESE
1 CUP SHREDDED MONTEREY JACK CHEESE

1. Combine the chicken, onion, garlic, celery, carrots, Alfredo sauce, and poultry seasoning in the slow cooker. Cover and cook on low for 7 to 8 hours.

2. Add the peas to the slow cooker; cover and cook on low for 1 more hour.

3. When you're ready to eat, preheat the oven to 400°F.

4. Cut the pie crust into four wedges and place them on a cookie sheet. Sprinkle each wedge with the Parmesan cheese. Bake the wedges for 9 to 12 minutes or until they are light golden brown. Cool on a wire rack.

5. Stir the Monterey Jack cheese into the chicken mixture, and let stand for 5 minutes until the cheese melts.

6. Spoon the chicken mixture into bowls and top each serving with the pie crust wedges.

Creamy Chicken with Penne

SERVES 2

Prep time: 15 minutes
Cook time: 5 hours

Penne pasta is named after the Latin word for "quill." It's shaped like a hollow cylinder with pointed ends. This pasta is thicker than spaghetti, so it needs to be partially cooked before being added to the sauce in the slow cooker to make it tender. This creamy and comforting recipe is delicious served with a crisp green salad and some toasted garlic bread.

¾ CUP PENNE PASTA

1 TABLESPOON EXTRA-VIRGIN OLIVE OIL

½ CUP MINCED ONION

6 BUTTON MUSHROOMS, SLICED

1 CUP PREPARED ALFREDO SAUCE (FROM A 16-OUNCE JAR)

½ CUP LOW-SODIUM CHICKEN BROTH

¼ CUP SOUR CREAM

2 BONELESS, SKINLESS CHICKEN BREASTS, CUBED

½ CUP FROZEN BABY PEAS

¾ CUP SHREDDED SWISS CHEESE

2 TABLESPOONS GRATED PARMESAN CHEESE

1. Bring a small pot of water to a boil. Add the pasta and cook for half of the shortest cooking time directed on the package; drain the pasta and set aside.

2. In a small skillet over medium heat, heat the olive oil. Add the onion and mushrooms; cook and stir for 4 to 5 minutes or until tender.

3. In the slow cooker, combine the pasta, onion mixture, Alfredo sauce, broth, and sour cream and mix well. Stir in the chicken.

4. Cover and cook on low for 4 hours; stir. Add the peas; cover and cook on low for 1 more hour or until the chicken registers 160°F on an instant-read thermometer and the pasta is tender.

5. Stir in the Swiss cheese. Serve sprinkled with Parmesan cheese.

Coq au Vin

Prep time: 15 minutes
Cook time: 7½ hours

Coq au vin sounds fancy, but it's just chicken cooked in red wine with vegetables. The rich sauce is delicious served over hot cooked rice or mashed potatoes. When you're cooking with wine, use a good-quality wine that you would enjoy drinking. The flavor of the wine concentrates in the slow cooker, so make sure it's delicious!

½ CUP DRY RED WINE

1 CUP LOW-SODIUM CHICKEN BROTH

2 TABLESPOONS TOMATO PASTE

½ TEASPOON DRIED OREGANO

½ TEASPOON SALT

⅛ TEASPOON FRESHLY GROUND WHITE PEPPER

1 POUND BONELESS, SKINLESS CHICKEN THIGHS

½ CUP CHOPPED ONION

1 CARROT, PEELED AND SLICED

6 BUTTON MUSHROOMS, SLICED

2 GARLIC CLOVES, MINCED

1 TABLESPOON CORNSTARCH

1. Combine the wine, ¾ cup of broth, tomato paste, and oregano in the slow cooker and stir to dissolve the tomato paste.

2. Sprinkle the salt and pepper over the chicken and place it in the slow cooker. Add the onion, carrot, mushrooms, and garlic, and stir.

3. Cover and cook on low for 6 to 7 hours or until the chicken registers 160°F on an instant-read thermometer.

4. In a small bowl, whisk together the cornstarch and the remaining ¼ cup of broth; add the mixture to the slow cooker. Cover and cook on high for 15 to 20 minutes or until the sauce thickens. Serve hot.

Greek Chicken Sandwiches

SERVES 2 TO 3

Prep time: 15 minutes
Cook time: 6 hours

Making sandwich fillings in the slow cooker is easy. You can flavor them in many ways, using spices and ingredients from Italian, Greek, Tex-Mex, and German cuisines. This filling is Greek because it uses artichoke hearts, olives, and feta cheese. You can find focaccia rolls in most bakeries.

Canned artichoke hearts used to be a luxury item, but now they're found in the regular grocery store. They are a lot of work to make from scratch: the artichokes are cooked, the leaves and choke are removed, and the heart is then cut into quarters. You can find them plain, packed in liquid, or marinated in a spicy dressing. Any kind will work in this recipe. You can put the remaining half a can in a green salad for your next meal.

1 POUND BONELESS, SKINLESS CHICKEN THIGHS

½ CUP CHOPPED ONION

2 GARLIC CLOVES, MINCED

HALF OF 14-OUNCE CAN ARTICHOKE HEARTS, DRAINED

2 TABLESPOONS LOW-SODIUM CHICKEN BROTH

½ TEASPOON DRIED OREGANO

3 TABLESPOONS CHOPPED BLACK OLIVES

⅓ CUP MAYONNAISE

3 TABLESPOONS CRUMBLED FETA CHEESE

2 OR 3 LARGE FOCACCIA OR CIABATTA ROLLS, SPLIT AND TOASTED

1. Combine the chicken, onion, garlic, artichoke hearts, broth, and oregano in the slow cooker. Cover and cook on low for 6 hours, until the chicken is tender and registers 160°F on an instant-read thermometer.

2. Remove the chicken from the slow cooker and shred it, using two forks. Return the chicken to the slow cooker and add the olives; stir gently to combine.

3. Make sandwiches with the mayonnaise, chicken mixture, cheese, and rolls.

Butter Chicken

SERVES 2

Prep time: 15 minutes
Cook time: 7½ hours

Butter chicken sounds rich, but there's no butter in it! The name comes from the velvety softness of the chicken when it's slowly cooked in the tomato sauce. This flavorful recipe is wonderful served over hot cooked brown or white rice. Use more or less curry powder to suit your taste.

4 BONELESS, SKINLESS CHICKEN THIGHS, CUT INTO 1-INCH PIECES

½ CUP CHOPPED ONION

1 GARLIC CLOVE, MINCED

1 TO 2 TEASPOONS CURRY POWDER

1 TEASPOON YELLOW CURRY PASTE

½ TEASPOON SALT

⅛ TEASPOON FRESHLY GROUND WHITE PEPPER

3 TABLESPOONS TOMATO PASTE

1 TABLESPOON FRESHLY SQUEEZED LEMON JUICE

1 TEASPOON FINELY MINCED GINGER ROOT

½ CUP COCONUT MILK

¾ CUP LOW-SODIUM CHICKEN BROTH

⅓ CUP PLAIN YOGURT

2 TEASPOONS CORNSTARCH

1. Combine all the ingredients except the yogurt and cornstarch in the slow cooker.

2. Cover and cook on low for 6 to 7 hours, or until the chicken is tender and registers 160°F on an instant-read thermometer.

3. In a small bowl, whisk together the yogurt and cornstarch. Stir the mixture into the slow cooker.

4. Cover and cook on high for 15 to 20 minutes or until sauce is thickened. Serve over hot cooked rice.

Lasagna Chicken Rollups

SERVES 2

Prep time: 20 minutes
Cook time: 4 hours

Lasagna noodles make a delicious and beautiful entrée when filled and rolled up. They nestle quite nicely into the slow cooker. This recipe is quite mild, but you could make it spicier by adding a pinch or two of red pepper flakes. You can use chicken thighs or breasts for this recipe; they just have to be precooked.

4 LASAGNA NOODLES

½ CUP RICOTTA CHEESE

ONE 3-OUNCE PACKAGE CREAM CHEESE, AT ROOM TEMPERATURE

1 CUP DICED COOKED CHICKEN

2 TABLESPOONS GRATED PARMESAN CHEESE

1 TEASPOON MINCED FRESH CHIVES

½ TEASPOON DRIED ITALIAN SEASONING

1½ CUPS SPAGHETTI SAUCE

1 CUP SHREDDED MOZZARELLA CHEESE

1. Cook the noodles in boiling water according to package directions. Drain well and place them on a kitchen towel; let cool for 10 minutes.

2. Meanwhile, in a small bowl, combine the ricotta cheese, cream cheese, chicken, Parmesan cheese, chives, and Italian seasoning.

3. Place the lasagna noodles on a work surface. Divide the chicken mixture among the noodles. Roll up, enclosing the filling.

4. Place ½ cup of spaghetti sauce in the slow cooker. Place the rolled lasagna noodles, seam-side down, in the sauce. Spoon the remaining sauce on and around the noodles.

5. Cover and cook on low for 3 to 4 hours, or until the mixture is heated through. Sprinkle the rollups with the mozzarella cheese; cover and cook on low for 10 minutes longer until the cheese melts. Serve immediately.

Chicken Cacciatore

Prep time: 15 minutes
Cook time: 6 hours

Cacciatore *means "hunter" in Italian. Chicken cacciatore, therefore, is chicken cooked in a hunter style. This just means that the ingredients are hearty and rich, including tomatoes, onions, and herbs. Serve this flavorful recipe with hot cooked spaghetti or fettuccine noodles tossed with a little butter just before serving.*

2 BONE-IN, SKINLESS CHICKEN BREASTS
2 TABLESPOONS ALL-PURPOSE FLOUR
½ TEASPOON SALT
⅛ TEASPOON FRESHLY GROUND BLACK PEPPER
½ CUP CHOPPED ONION
2 GARLIC CLOVES, MINCED
6 BUTTON MUSHROOMS, CHOPPED
¼ CUP DRY WHITE WINE
¼ CUP LOW-SODIUM CHICKEN BROTH
ONE 14-OUNCE CAN DICED TOMATOES, UNDRAINED
2 TABLESPOONS TOMATO PASTE
½ TEASPOON DRIED OREGANO

1. Sprinkle the chicken with the flour, salt, and pepper.

2. Combine the onion, garlic, and mushrooms in the slow cooker; top with the chicken.

3. In a small bowl, whisk together the wine, broth, tomatoes, tomato paste, and oregano. Pour the mixture into the slow cooker.

4. Cover and cook on low for 5 to 6 hours or until the chicken registers 160°F on an instant-read thermometer. Serve over hot cooked pasta.

Sticky Chicken

SERVES 2

Prep time: 15 minutes
Cook time: 5 hours

Sticky chicken really does stick to your fingers, making this a messy and fun meal. The ingredients combine to form a glaze on the chicken as it cooks. While flavorful, this recipe isn't very spicy, so it's good for more timid palates. Serve it with some mashed potatoes, a chopped vegetable salad, and a bakery pie for dessert.

½ CUP MINCED ONION

2 GARLIC CLOVES, MINCED

⅓ CUP FRESHLY SQUEEZED ORANGE JUICE

¼ CUP HONEY

3 TABLESPOONS PACKED BROWN SUGAR

2 TABLESPOONS SOY SAUCE

1 TABLESPOON FRESHLY SQUEEZED LEMON JUICE

3 BONELESS, SKINLESS CHICKEN BREASTS

1. In a small saucepan over medium heat, combine all ingredients except the chicken and bring to a boil.

2. Lower the heat and simmer for 5 minutes until the sauce starts to thicken. Pour the sauce into the slow cooker.

3. Add the chicken and turn with tongs to coat the meat in the sauce.

4. Cover and cook on low for 3 to 5 hours or until the chicken registers 160°F on an instant-read thermometer. Serve with lots of napkins!

Chicken Enchiladas

Prep time: 15 minutes
Cook time: 4 hours

You can buy enchilada sauce in cans or jars at the regular grocery store. It comes in mild, medium, and hot spice levels. If you can't find it, you can substitute smooth taco sauce. And you can use flour or corn tortillas in this recipe. Corn tortillas are usually smaller, with a more robust flavor.

1 TABLESPOON EXTRA-VIRGIN OLIVE OIL

½ CUP CHOPPED ONION

2 GARLIC CLOVES, MINCED

½ JALAPEÑO PEPPER, MINCED

1½ CUPS DICED COOKED CHICKEN

1 CUP ENCHILADA SAUCE

1 TO 2 TEASPOONS CHILI POWDER

⅓ CUP SOUR CREAM, PLUS MORE FOR SERVING

5 TORTILLAS

1 CUP SHREDDED PEPPER JACK CHEESE

GUACAMOLE, FOR SERVING (OPTIONAL)

1. In a small skillet over medium heat, heat the olive oil. Add the onion and garlic; cook and stir until tender, about 4 minutes. Add the jalapeño; cook and stir for 1 minute longer.

2. Remove the pan from the heat and add the chicken, ¼ cup of enchilada sauce, chili powder, and sour cream; mix well.

3. Place the tortillas on a work surface. Divide the chicken mixture among the tortillas. Top each with 1 tablespoon of pepper Jack cheese and roll up.

4. Place ¼ cup of enchilada sauce on the bottom of the slow cooker. Top with the filled enchiladas, seam-side down. Pour the remaining ½ cup of enchilada sauce over all. Sprinkle with the remaining pepper Jack cheese.

5. Cover and cook on low for 3 to 4 hours or until the mixture is hot and bubbly. Serve with guacamole (if using) and more sour cream.

Chicken Mole

SERVES 2

Prep time: 15 minutes
Cook time: 8 hours

Mole sauce comes from Mexico. It's made from onions, garlic, tomatoes, spices, and dark chocolate. The sauce doesn't taste sweet; the chocolate adds a smoky taste and wonderful depth of flavor. Serve this recipe with guacamole and chips to start, and a fresh fruit salad to cool your palate.

5 BONELESS, SKINLESS CHICKEN THIGHS

ONE 14-OUNCE CAN DICED TOMATOES, UNDRAINED

½ DRIED ANCHO CHILE, CRUMBLED

½ CUP MINCED ONION

2 GARLIC CLOVES, PEELED

2 TABLESPOONS ADOBO SAUCE

1 TABLESPOON MINCED BITTERSWEET CHOCOLATE

2 TABLESPOONS PEANUT BUTTER

2 TABLESPOONS DRIED CURRANTS

1 TEASPOON CHILI POWDER

½ TEASPOON GROUND CUMIN

¼ TEASPOON GROUND CINNAMON

1. Place the chicken thighs in the slow cooker.

2. In a blender, combine the remaining ingredients and blend well. Pour the mixture over the chicken and stir.

3. Cover and cook on low for 7 to 8 hours or until the chicken is tender and registers 160°F on an instant-read thermometer. Serve over hot cooked rice.

CHAPTER NINE

Meat

Savory, hearty dishes made with beef, pork, and lamb are delicious and easy to put together in the slow cooker. When they are cooked in liquid at a low temperature over a long period of time—a technique called "braising"—these meats develop a rich flavor and tender texture. And ground meats can be combined with anything from peanut butter to potatoes and wine to great effect.

For richer flavor and a caramelized exterior, brown whole cuts of meat before you add them to the slow cooker. Whole cuts of meat include beef roasts and steaks; pork chops, roasts, and tenderloin; and leg of lamb and lamb shoulder. The whole cuts of beef used in slow cooker recipes cook to about 200°F, so they become very tender. Pork is cooked to a lower temperature because it has very little connective tissue that needs to soften.

Enjoy these rich and simple recipes, perhaps accompanied by one of the side dishes in Chapter Six.

SWISS STEAK	BEEF BOURGUIGNON
PORK IN PEANUT SAUCE	CHEESY STUFFED MEAT LOAF
GLAZED HAM SANDWICHES	TACO SALAD
PORK CHOPS WITH RED CABBAGE	BEEF STROGANOFF
SAUSAGE AND PEPPERS	SAVORY LEG OF LAMB

Swiss Steak

SERVES 2

Prep time: 15 minutes
Cook time: 8 hours

Top or bottom round steak is the cut to choose when making this recipe. The steak is pounded before it is cooked to help break apart fibers and to force seasonings into the meat. Use a meat mallet or a rolling pin for this task. (Make sure you wash the mallet or pin well after using it!)

½ POUND ROUND STEAK, CUT INTO 2 PIECES
2 TABLESPOONS ALL-PURPOSE FLOUR
½ TEASPOON SALT
FRESHLY GROUND BLACK PEPPER
½ TEASPOON DRIED MARJORAM
1 TABLESPOON EXTRA-VIRGIN OLIVE OIL
½ CUP CHOPPED ONION
2 GARLIC CLOVES, MINCED
1 CUP LOW-SODIUM BEEF BROTH
2 TABLESPOONS TOMATO PASTE
1 TEASPOON WORCESTERSHIRE SAUCE
2 TOMATOES, CHOPPED

1. Sprinkle the steaks with the flour, salt, pepper, and marjoram on both sides. Using a meat mallet, pound this mixture into the steaks.

2. In a medium skillet over medium-high heat, heat the olive oil. Brown the steaks, turning once, for about 5 minutes total. Transfer the steaks to the slow cooker.

3. Add the onion and garlic to the drippings in the skillet and turn the heat down to medium; cook for 4 minutes. Add the broth and bring to a simmer, scraping up the brown bits from the bottom of the pan. Add the tomato paste and Worcestershire sauce, mix well, and pour the mixture over the steak in the slow cooker.

4. Add the tomatoes to the slow cooker. Cover and cook on low for 7 to 8 hours or until the meat is tender.

Pork in Peanut Sauce

Prep time: 15 minutes
Cook time: 7 hours

Peanut butter is often used in Thai cooking to add richness and body to sauces. If you can't eat peanuts, almond butter and other nut butters also work well. Rice vinegar is used in this style of cooking, too; if you don't have it on hand, you can substitute white wine vinegar or apple cider vinegar. Serve with cooked rice to soak up the sauce.

. . . .

Pork tenderloin is a specific cut of pork that looks like a long tube. Like beef tenderloin, it is the most tender part of the animal. The tenderloin is not a pork roast. It's usually wrapped and sold in the meat section of the supermarket. If you don't see it, ask the butcher for it. This lean cut of meat cooks well in the slow cooker and can be flavored many ways.

. . . .

ONE 1-POUND PORK TENDERLOIN

½ CUP CHOPPED ONION

1 GARLIC CLOVE, MINCED

1 TEASPOON MINCED FRESH GINGER ROOT

¼ CUP PEANUT BUTTER

½ CUP LOW-SODIUM CHICKEN BROTH

2 TABLESPOONS RICE VINEGAR

2 TABLESPOONS TERIYAKI SAUCE

2 TABLESPOONS PACKED BROWN SUGAR

1 TABLESPOON SOY SAUCE

1. Place the pork in the slow cooker.

2. In a small microwave-safe bowl, combine the remaining ingredients. Microwave on high for 1 minute or until the peanut butter softens; stir to combine. Pour the mixture over the pork.

3. Cover and cook on low for 6 to 7 hours or until the pork is tender. Slice the pork and serve with the sauce.

Glazed Ham Sandwiches

SERVES 2 TO 3

Prep time: 15 minutes
Cook time: 4 hours

In this wonderful recipe, sliced ham is cooked in a sweet and spicy mixture of pineapple juice, mustard, and onion, then piled on kaiser or ciabatta rolls. The recipe makes more than enough to serve two people, but you will enjoy the leftovers. The ham shouldn't be sliced too thin; about 1/8 inch thick is ideal.

1 POUND SLICED HAM

¼ CUP PINEAPPLE JUICE

½ CUP CHOPPED ONION

¼ CUP PACKED BROWN SUGAR

2 TABLESPOONS HONEY

1 TABLESPOON DIJON MUSTARD

2 OR 3 KAISER OR CIABATTA ROLLS, SLICED AND TOASTED

1. Separate the ham slices and fold each one in half; place them in the slow cooker. In a small bowl, combine the remaining ingredients except the rolls, and pour the mixture over the ham.

2. Cover and cook on low for 4 hours or until the mixture is heated through. Make sandwiches with the ham and the rolls; drizzle with the liquid from the slow cooker.

Pork Chops with Red Cabbage

SERVES 2

Prep time: 20 minutes

Cook time: 7 hours

Red cabbage is often served with pork in Germany. The sweet and sour vegetable complements the tender and mild pork. Choose boneless, thick-cut pork chops for this recipe. Trim off any excess fat and brown the chops quickly, just to add a little color and flavor to this hearty recipe.

TWO 6-OUNCE BONELESS CENTER-CUT PORK LOIN CHOPS

1 TABLESPOON EXTRA-VIRGIN OLIVE OIL

½ CUP CHOPPED ONION

1 GARLIC CLOVE, MINCED

2½ CUPS SHREDDED RED CABBAGE

¼ CUP PEELED CHOPPED APPLE

2 TABLESPOONS DRIED CRANBERRIES

2 TABLESPOONS PACKED BROWN SUGAR

¼ CUP APPLE CIDER VINEGAR

½ TEASPOON DRIED MARJORAM

1. In a small skillet, brown the pork chops in olive oil over medium heat, turning once, for about 4 minutes total.

2. Remove the chops from the skillet and set aside. Add the onion and garlic to the skillet; cook for 3 minutes, stirring to include the drippings.

3. Combine the onion mixture, cabbage, apple, and cranberries in the slow cooker.

4. In a small bowl, combine the brown sugar, vinegar, and marjoram; add this mixture to the cabbage mixture and stir. Top with the pork chops.

5. Cover and cook on low for 7 hours or until the pork and cabbage are tender. Serve hot.

Sausage and Peppers

SERVES 2

Prep time: 15 minutes
Cook time: 6 hours

Here's a classic Italian dish made in slow-cooker style. You can use sweet or hot Italian sausages, or try bratwurst or Polish sausages. If you use uncooked sausages, brown them in a skillet before you put them in the slow cooker to reduce the fat and add flavor and color to the finished dish.

. . . .

Sausages are made of ground pork or other meats combined with spices. The uncooked varieties of sausage include bratwurst, Italian sausages, andouille, boudin blanc, bockwurst, and Polish sausage. The cooked varieties of sausage include kielbasa, salami, summer sausage, linguica, chorizo, and bologna. The package will indicate whether the sausage is fully cooked and ready to eat, or if it should be cooked to 160°F before serving.

. . . .

¾ POUND HOT OR SWEET ITALIAN SAUSAGES

⅔ CUP DRY RED WINE OR LOW-SODIUM BEEF BROTH

3 TABLESPOONS TOMATO PASTE

½ CUP CHOPPED ONION

1 GARLIC CLOVE, MINCED

1 RED BELL PEPPER, THINLY SLICED

½ GREEN BELL PEPPER, THINLY SLICED

2 TOMATOES, CHOPPED

½ TEASPOON DRIED OREGANO

1. Prick the sausages with a fork, then cook them in a small skillet in a small amount of water until browned, turning occasionally, about 10 minutes. Remove the sausages and set aside. Add the wine and tomato paste to the skillet, scraping up any brown bits from the bottom of the pan.

2. Place the onion and garlic in the slow cooker and top them with the sausages. Add the peppers, tomatoes, and oregano, and then pour in the wine mixture from the skillet.

3. Cover and cook on low for 5 to 6 hours or until the sausages register 165°F on an instant-read thermometer.

Beef Bourguignon

Prep time: 15 minutes
Cook time: 7 hours

Beef Bourguignon is a classic French dish made of cubes of beef cooked in wine. The recipe is very rich and should be served over hot cooked egg noodles. Any cut of beef will work well in this recipe, but don't use the cubed beef sold as stew meat. Try sirloin or bottom round and cut it into cubes yourself.

2 SLICES BACON
½ CUP CHOPPED ONION
2 GARLIC CLOVES, MINCED
8 BUTTON MUSHROOMS, SLICED
½ CUP LOW-SODIUM BEEF BROTH
1 CUP DRY RED WINE
2 TABLESPOONS TOMATO PASTE
½ POUND SIRLOIN STEAK, CUT INTO 1-INCH CUBES
½ TEASPOON SALT
FRESHLY GROUND BLACK PEPPER
½ TEASPOON DRIED MARJORAM
1 TABLESPOON CORNSTARCH
3 TABLESPOONS WATER

1. In a small skillet over medium heat, cook the bacon until crisp. Drain the bacon on paper towels, crumble, and set aside.

2. Cook the onion, garlic, and mushrooms in the bacon drippings in the skillet for 3 to 4 minutes until crisp-tender. Add the broth, wine, and tomato paste and stir well. Place this mixture in the slow cooker.

3. Sprinkle the steak with the salt, pepper, and marjoram, and add it to the slow cooker along with the bacon.

4. Cover and cook on low for 6 to 7 hours or until beef is tender.

5. In a small bowl, whisk together the cornstarch and water. Stir the mixture into the slow cooker; cover and cook on high for 10 to 15 minutes or until the sauce thickens. Serve over hot cooked egg noodles.

Cheesy Stuffed Meat Loaf

SERVES 2

Prep time: 15 minutes
Cook time: 4 hours

Meat loaf is easy to make in the slow cooker. Be sure that you use a foil sling as directed on page 8 to remove the meat loaf easily when it is done. One of the secrets to making meat loaf is to let it stand for a few minutes after it's done cooking. You can use any type of cheese to stuff this meat loaf; your favorite variety will work well.

1 TABLESPOON UNSALTED BUTTER
⅓ CUP MINCED ONION
1 GARLIC CLOVE, MINCED
1 TABLESPOON CHILI SAUCE
¼ TEASPOON SALT
PINCH OF FRESHLY GROUND BLACK PEPPER
1 EGG
¼ CUP SOFT BREAD CRUMBS
¼ POUND LEAN GROUND BEEF
¼ POUND GROUND PORK
ONE 1-BY-4-INCH RECTANGLE HAVARTI CHEESE
1 CUP SPAGHETTI SAUCE
3 TABLESPOONS GRATED PARMESAN CHEESE

1. In a small skillet over medium heat, melt the butter. Add the onion and garlic; cook until tender, 5 to 6 minutes. Remove the skillet from the heat and transfer the mixture to a medium bowl.

2. Add the chili sauce, salt, pepper, egg, and bread crumbs to the onion mixture and mix well. Add the beef and pork and mix gently but thoroughly with a rubber spatula.

3. Place half of the meat mixture in the slow cooker in a 5-by-3-inch rectangle. Top with the Havarti cheese. Form the remaining meat mixture around the cheese and seal the sides.

4. Pour the spaghetti sauce over the meat loaf and sprinkle it with the Parmesan cheese.

5. Cover and cook on high for 3 to 4 hours or until the meat loaf registers 165°F on an instant-read thermometer. Remove the meat loaf from the slow cooker using the foil sling, tent with foil, and let stand for 5 minutes before slicing.

Taco Salad

Prep time: 15 minutes
Cook time: 5 hours

This spicy, savory, warm-and-cool salad has the perfect combination of textures and flavors. You can use a bagged salad for the greens, or choose your own combination of lettuces, including romaine, arugula, and red leaf. Top the taco salad with your choice of ingredients, such as chopped olives, guacamole, chopped tomato, sour cream, and shredded cheese.

½ POUND GROUND BEEF

½ CUP CHOPPED ONION

1 GARLIC CLOVE, MINCED

1½ CUPS THICK SALSA

1 TEASPOON CHILI POWDER

¼ TEASPOON GROUND CUMIN

⅛ TEASPOON FRESHLY GROUND BLACK PEPPER

4 CUPS MIXED LETTUCE GREENS

1 RED BELL PEPPER, CHOPPED

½ CUP CORN CHIPS

½ CUP SHREDDED CHEDDAR CHEESE

AVOCADO, SOUR CREAM, AND MORE SALSA, FOR TOPPING (OPTIONAL)

1. In a small skillet over medium heat, cook the ground beef with the onion and garlic, stirring to break up the meat, for about 5 minutes or until the beef is browned. Drain well.

2. Combine the meat mixture with the salsa, chili powder, cumin, and pepper in the slow cooker. Cover and cook on low for 4 to 5 hours or until blended.

3. To serve, place the lettuce, bell pepper, and corn chips on plates. Top with the beef mixture. Sprinkle with Cheddar cheese and assorted toppings (if using).

Beef Stroganoff

SERVES 2

Prep time: 15 minutes
Cook time: 7½ hours

Beef stroganoff is made of beef, onions, and mushrooms cooked in a rich sauce thickened with sour cream. It is delicious served over hot rice or hot cooked egg noodles. Sirloin tip is the best cut to use for this easy recipe. Serve it with a green salad, some cooked carrots, and a nice red wine.

½ POUND BEEF SIRLOIN TIP, CUBED

½ CUP MINCED ONION

1 GARLIC CLOVE, MINCED

6 SMALL BUTTON MUSHROOMS, LEFT WHOLE

½ TEASPOON SALT

FRESHLY GROUND BLACK PEPPER

½ TEASPOON DRIED MARJORAM

¼ TEASPOON GROUND MUSTARD

1 BAY LEAF

1 CUP LOW-SODIUM BEEF BROTH

½ CUP DRY RED WINE

2 TEASPOONS WORCESTERSHIRE SAUCE

½ CUP SOUR CREAM

1 TABLESPOON ALL-PURPOSE FLOUR

1. In the slow cooker, combine the beef, onion, garlic, mushrooms, salt, pepper, marjoram, and mustard. Top with the bay leaf.

2. Pour the broth, wine, and Worcestershire sauce into the slow cooker. Cover and cook on low for 7 hours until the meat is very tender. Remove and discard the bay leaf.

3. In a small bowl, combine the sour cream and flour. Add about ½ cup of liquid from the slow cooker and mix well. Stir this mixture back into the slow cooker.

4. Cover and cook on high for 20 to 25 minutes or until the mixture thickens. Serve over hot cooked egg noodles.

Savory Leg of Lamb

SERVES 2

Prep time: 15 minutes
Cook time: 8 hours

Leg of lamb is a meaty and tender cut. Lamb has a lot of fat, so this meat should be browned before you add it to the slow cooker. Because the meat is so rich, it is usually served with an accompaniment such as mint or red currant jelly to cut through the fat. You may need to ask the butcher for a piece of lamb this size, as a boneless leg of lamb is usually much larger, about 2 to 3 pounds.

1 POUND BONELESS LEG OF LAMB ROAST
2 GARLIC CLOVES, PEELED AND SLIVERED
1 TABLESPOON EXTRA-VIRGIN OLIVE OIL
⅛ TEASPOON SALT
⅛ TEASPOON FRESHLY GROUND BLACK PEPPER
½ TEASPOON DRIED THYME
¼ TEASPOON DRIED BASIL
1 LEMON, THINLY SLICED
½ CUP WATER

1. Using a sharp knife, cut about 20 slits in the lamb. Push the garlic slivers into each slit.

2. In a medium skillet over medium heat, heat the olive oil. Add the lamb and brown well on all sides, about 10 minutes.

3. Place the lamb in the slow cooker and sprinkle it with salt, pepper, thyme, and basil. Cover the lamb with the lemon slices. Pour the water into the slow cooker.

4. Cover and cook on low for 7 to 8 hours or until the meat is very tender. Remove the lamb from the slow cooker. Tent the lamb with foil and let it stand for 10 minutes, then slice it thinly to serve.

CHAPTER TEN

One-Pot Meals

One-pot meals combine the main dish and a side dish for two-in-one convenience. For instance, you'll be able to serve a pot roast with vegetables, a complete main dish salad, or turkey with stuffing from one pot! A few of these recipes use cooking bags in a fun way. You'll cook the main dish in one bag and the side dish in another bag. All these recipes need is a lettuce or fruit salad to create a complete meal.

Substitutions will work well in many of these recipes. For instance, in the recipe for Meat Loaf with Potatoes, use a combination of ground beef and pork sausage, and try using sliced sweet potatoes in place of the russet potatoes. In the recipe for Chili over Sweet Potatoes, use regular potatoes, and use ground turkey instead of the ground pork. You can also vary the spices, using more or less according to your taste.

Another benefit to one-pot meals is that cleanup is easy. You can use cooking bags to make any of these recipes. When you have eaten, just throw away the bag, wash out the slow cooker insert, and you're done.

ITALIAN POT ROAST

SHORT RIBS WITH POLENTA

RICH LASAGNA

CHILI OVER SWEET POTATOES

HOT GERMAN POTATO SALAD

MEAT LOAF WITH POTATOES

TURKEY AND SWEET POTATOES

BARLEY-WILD RICE CHICKEN SALAD

BEEFY SPAGHETTI

TAMALE PIE

TURKEY WITH STUFFING

CASSOULET

Italian Pot Roast

SERVES 2

Prep time: 15 minutes
Cook time: 9 hours

Pot roast is made using an inexpensive cut of beef that cooks for a long time so the meat becomes very tender and moist. The flavors in this easy recipe are reminiscent of Italy, including basil, oregano, garlic, onion, and wine. Serve with some nice red wine for a comforting meal.

1 POUND CHUCK OR BOTTOM ROUND ROAST
½ TEASPOON SALT
½ TEASPOON DRIED BASIL
¼ TEASPOON DRIED OREGANO
2 SMALL RUSSET POTATOES, PEELED AND CUT INTO CHUNKS
1 CARROT, SLICED
1 SUN-DRIED TOMATO IN OIL, DRAINED AND CHOPPED
½ CUP CHOPPED ONION
2 GARLIC CLOVES, MINCED
½ CUP LOW-SODIUM BEEF BROTH
¼ CUP DRY RED WINE
1 TABLESPOON TOMATO PASTE

1. Sprinkle the meat with the salt, basil, and oregano.

2. Place the potatoes, carrot, tomato, onion, and garlic in the slow cooker. Top with the roast.

3. In a small bowl, combine the broth, wine, and tomato paste and mix well. Pour the mixture over the meat.

4. Cover and cook on low for 8 to 9 hours or until the meat is very tender.

5. Slice the meat against the grain and serve with the vegetables and the sauce.

Short Ribs with Polenta

SERVES 2

Prep time: 25 minutes

Cook time: 8 hours

Beef short ribs are a boneless, inexpensive cut that, when cooked, produce a rich gravy that is delicious served over polenta. Two cooking bags are used for this recipe. Make sure you buy bags made for the slow cooker. The polenta does need to be stirred once during the cooking time; just open that bag and stir, then replace the lid.

- -

Polenta is coarse-ground cornmeal. It may be labeled as "polenta" or "cornmeal" on the package. The best cornmeal for polenta is medium or coarse ground. Don't use masa harina, which is a finely ground product used to make tortillas and tamales. And for use in the slow cooker, don't buy quick-cooking or instant polenta, which will overcook and become very mushy.

- -

¾ POUND BONELESS BEEF RIBS

2 TABLESPOONS ALL-PURPOSE FLOUR

½ TEASPOON SALT

FRESHLY GROUND BLACK PEPPER

½ TEASPOON DRIED MARJORAM

2 TABLESPOONS EXTRA-VIRGIN OLIVE OIL

½ CUP CHOPPED ONION

2 GARLIC CLOVES, MINCED

¼ CUP LOW-SODIUM BEEF BROTH

¼ CUP KETCHUP

2 TABLESPOONS PACKED BROWN SUGAR

2 TABLESPOONS BALSAMIC VINEGAR

2 TABLESPOONS TOMATO PASTE

1 CUP LOW-SODIUM CHICKEN BROTH

½ CUP WATER

½ CUP POLENTA (NOT THE QUICK-COOKING VARIETY)

½ TEASPOON SALT

1 TABLESPOON UNSALTED BUTTER, MELTED

continued ▶

1. Coat the ribs with the flour, salt, pepper, and marjoram.

2. In a medium skillet over medium heat, heat the olive oil. Add the ribs and brown them, turning occasionally, for about 5 minutes. After the meat browns, put it into a cooking bag.

3. When all the meat is browned and in the bag, add the onion and garlic to the skillet; cook for 2 to 3 minutes. Add the beef broth, ketchup, brown sugar, vinegar, and tomato paste and bring to a simmer. Pour the mixture over the meat in the cooking bag.

4. Arrange the cooking bag so that it fits in one half of the slow cooker. Place another cooking bag next to the bag with the ribs. Add the chicken broth, water, polenta, salt, and butter and stir well.

5. Cover the slow cooker and cook on low for 7 to 8 hours or until the beef is tender and the polenta is hot and cooked. Stir the polenta once or twice during the cooking time. Serve the beef mixture over the polenta.

Rich Lasagna

SERVES 2

Prep time: 15 minutes
Cook time: 7 hours

No-boil noodles make cooking lasagna much easier. They are perfect for the slow cooker because they will absorb liquid and cook slowly without becoming too soft. The no-boil noodles usually don't have the curly edges that traditional lasagna noodles have.

½ POUND SWEET ITALIAN SAUSAGE, CASINGS REMOVED

½ CUP CHOPPED ONION

1 GARLIC CLOVE, MINCED

1 TOMATO, DICED

ONE 8-OUNCE CAN TOMATO SAUCE

2 TABLESPOONS TOMATO PASTE

½ CUP WATER

⅔ CUP RICOTTA CHEESE

1 OUNCE CREAM CHEESE, AT ROOM TEMPERATURE

1 EGG, BEATEN

1½ CUPS SHREDDED MOZZARELLA CHEESE

4 NO-BOIL LASAGNA NOODLES

¼ CUP GRATED PARMESAN CHEESE

1. In a medium skillet over medium heat, cook the sausage with the onion and garlic, stirring to break up the meat, until the meat is no longer pink. Drain well.

2. Add the tomato, tomato sauce, tomato paste, and water to the skillet and bring to a simmer; simmer for 2 minutes. Remove the pan from the heat and let it cool for 10 minutes.

3. In a small bowl, combine the ricotta, cream cheese, egg, and ½ cup of mozzarella cheese; mix well.

4. Place ¼ cup of sauce in the bottom of the slow cooker. Add one layer of noodles. Top with a third of the sauce, a third of the ricotta mixture, and a third of the remaining mozzarella cheese. Repeat the layers, ending with the mozzarella. Sprinkle with the Parmesan cheese.

5. Cover and cook on low for 6 to 7 hours or until the noodles are tender. Let the lasagna cool slightly before serving.

Chili over Sweet Potatoes

SERVES 2

Prep time: 15 minutes
Cook time: 7 hours

The sweet potatoes cook all by themselves in this easy recipe, while the chili cooks in a cooking bag. When both are done, you cut the sweet potatoes in half and layer the chili on top. This comforting and rich recipe is delicious served with a fruit salad to cut the heat and a cold bottle of beer.

½ POUND GROUND PORK

½ CUP CHOPPED ONION

1 GARLIC CLOVE, MINCED

1 SMALL JALAPEÑO PEPPER, MINCED

ONE 15-OUNCE CAN BLACK BEANS, RINSED AND DRAINED

2 TEASPOONS CHILI POWDER

½ TEASPOON GROUND CUMIN

¼ TEASPOON SALT

1 CUP LOW-SODIUM BEEF BROTH

½ CUP SALSA

2 SWEET POTATOES, SCRUBBED

SHREDDED CHEDDAR CHEESE, IF DESIRED

1. In a small skillet over medium heat, cook the ground pork with the onion and garlic, stirring to break up the meat, until the pork is no longer pink. Drain well.

2. Transfer the pork mixture to a cooking bag, along with the jalapeño, beans, chili powder, cumin, salt, broth, and salsa.

3. Prick the sweet potatoes with a fork and stack them in one half of the slow cooker. Nestle the bag with the chili ingredients next to the sweet potatoes.

4. Cover and cook on low for 7 hours, or until the sweet potatoes are tender and the chili is hot. Slice the sweet potatoes in half, place them on serving plates, and pour the chili over the potatoes. Sprinkle with cheese (if using).

Hot German Potato Salad

SERVES 2

Prep time: 15 minutes
Cook time: 6½ hours

German potato salad is served hot, unlike the American version. The potatoes are cooked with sausage in a sweet and sour dressing. Bacon adds a smoky note. The vinegar mixture is added at the end; otherwise, the acid would prevent the potatoes from softening.

2 SLICES BACON

1 BRATWURST SAUSAGE

½ CUP CHOPPED ONION

1 GARLIC CLOVE, MINCED

1 POUND SMALL RED POTATOES, CUT INTO QUARTERS

½ CUP LOW-SODIUM CHICKEN BROTH

3 TABLESPOONS SUGAR

3 TABLESPOONS APPLE CIDER VINEGAR

1 TABLESPOON CORNSTARCH

⅓ CUP SOUR CREAM

1. In a small skillet over medium heat, cook the bacon until crisp. Remove the bacon from the skillet; drain it on paper towels, crumble, and set aside.

2. Brown the sausage in the bacon drippings in the skillet over medium heat, turning frequently, 5 to 7 minutes. Slice the cooked sausage and set aside.

3. Combine the bacon, sausage, onion, garlic, and potatoes in the slow cooker and stir gently. Pour the broth over all.

4. Cover and cook on low for 5 to 6 hours or until the potatoes are tender.

5. In a small bowl, combine the sugar, vinegar, and cornstarch and stir the mixture into the slow cooker. Cover and cook on high for 15 to 20 minutes or until the sauce thickens. Stir in the sour cream and serve immediately.

Meat Loaf with Potatoes

SERVES 2

Prep time: 15 minutes
Cook time: 7 hours

A hearty and flavorful meat loaf cooks on a bed of potatoes in this one-pot meal. You could use sliced sweet potatoes, red potatoes, or Yukon Gold potatoes in place of the russets if you'd like. As the meat loaf cooks, the drippings flavor the potatoes.

1 TABLESPOON EXTRA-VIRGIN OLIVE OIL

⅓ CUP MINCED ONION

1 GARLIC CLOVE, MINCED

¼ CUP KETCHUP

1 TABLESPOON MUSTARD

¼ TEASPOON SALT

PINCH OF FRESHLY GROUND BLACK PEPPER

1 EGG

¼ CUP CRUSHED CORNFLAKES

½ POUND LEAN GROUND BEEF

2 MEDIUM RUSSET POTATOES, SLICED ½ INCH THICK

2 TABLESPOONS PACKED BROWN SUGAR

1. In a small skillet over medium heat, heat the olive oil. Add the onion and garlic; cook until tender, 5 to 6 minutes. Remove the skillet from the heat and transfer the onion-garlic mixture to a medium bowl.

2. Add ⅛ cup of ketchup, the mustard, salt, pepper, egg, and cornflakes to the onion mixture and mix well. Add the beef and mix gently but thoroughly with a rubber spatula.

3. Place the potato slices in the bottom of the slow cooker. Form the meat mixture into a loaf and place it on top of the potatoes.

4. In a small bowl, combine the remaining ⅛ cup of ketchup and the brown sugar. Spread the mixture over the meat loaf.

5. Cover and cook on high for 1 hour, then turn the slow cooker to low and cook about 5 to 6 hours longer, until the meat loaf registers 165°F on an instant-read thermometer. Remove the meat loaf from the slow cooker, cover with foil, and let stand 10 minutes before slicing. Serve with the potatoes.

Turkey and Sweet Potatoes

SERVES 2

Prep time: 15 minutes
Cook time: 7 hours

Turkey tenderloins are often sold in the meat department of the grocery store. If you don't see them, ask the butcher for one. They are tender and low in fat, and they cook well in the slow cooker. The combination of preserves, spices, and veggies in this one-pot dinner is delicious.

1 TURKEY TENDERLOIN, CUT INTO 1½-INCH CUBES

½ TEASPOON SALT

1 TEASPOON CURRY POWDER

2 SMALL SWEET POTATOES, PEELED AND CUBED

½ CUP CHOPPED ONION

1 CELERY STALK, CHOPPED

⅓ CUP APRICOT PRESERVES

1 TABLESPOON FRESHLY SQUEEZED LEMON JUICE

⅓ CUP LOW-SODIUM CHICKEN BROTH

1 TABLESPOON CORNSTARCH

3 TABLESPOONS WATER

1. Combine all the ingredients except the cornstarch and water in the slow cooker. Cover and cook on low for 7 hours or until the turkey and vegetables are tender.

2. In a small bowl, whisk together the cornstarch and water. Stir the mixture into the slow cooker. Cover and cook on high for 10 to 15 minutes, or until sauce thickens. Serve over hot cooked rice.

Barley–Wild Rice Chicken Salad

SERVES 2 TO 3

Prep time: 15 minutes
Cook time: 6 hours

Barley and wild rice cook for the same amount of time in the slow cooker. Add some chicken for a fabulous salad base. Just mix in a creamy mustard dressing and some fresh veggies for a wonderful main dish in the summer. The salad chills for a couple of hours in the fridge before it's ready to eat.

½ CUP PEARL BARLEY

½ CUP WILD RICE, RINSED

2 GARLIC CLOVES, MINCED

1 CUP LOW-SODIUM CHICKEN BROTH

2 CUPS WATER

4 BONELESS, SKINLESS CHICKEN THIGHS, CUBED

½ CUP MAYONNAISE

2 TABLESPOONS HONEY MUSTARD

1 TABLESPOON DIJON MUSTARD

1 TABLESPOON FRESHLY SQUEEZED LEMON JUICE

2 TABLESPOONS WHOLE MILK

1 ORANGE BELL PEPPER, CHOPPED

1 CELERY STALK, CHOPPED

1 CUP GRAPE TOMATOES

1. Combine the barley, rice, garlic, broth, water, and chicken thighs in the slow cooker. Cover and cook on low for 5 to 6 hours, or until the barley and rice are tender and the chicken registers 160°F on an instant-read thermometer. Drain if there is any excess liquid.

2. In a medium bowl, combine the mayonnaise, mustards, lemon juice, and milk and mix well. Stir in the mixture from the slow cooker. Then stir in the vegetables.

3. Cover and chill for 2 to 3 hours to blend flavors before serving. Store any leftover salad in the fridge for 3 to 5 days.

Beefy Spaghetti

Prep time: 15 minutes
Cook time: 6 hours

Ground beef is cooked in a rich tomato and vegetable sauce in this recipe. Serve it over hot cooked spaghetti, fettuccine, or linguine with some grated Parmesan cheese sprinkled on top. Garlic bread and a green salad are perfect accompaniments to this dish, as is a glass of good red wine.

½ POUND GROUND BEEF
½ CUP CHOPPED ONION
2 GARLIC CLOVES, MINCED
¼ CUP GRATED CARROT
1 CELERY STALK, CHOPPED
1 TOMATO, CHOPPED
ONE 8-OUNCE CAN TOMATO SAUCE
3 TABLESPOONS TOMATO PASTE
½ CUP WATER
½ TEASPOON DRIED ITALIAN SEASONING
8 OUNCES SPAGHETTI OR LINGUINE
¼ CUP GRATED PARMESAN CHEESE

1. In a small skillet over medium heat, cook the ground beef with the onion and garlic, stirring to break up the meat, until the beef is no longer pink, about 5 minutes. Drain well.

2. Combine the beef mixture, carrot, celery, and tomato in the slow cooker.

3. In the same skillet that you used for the beef, combine the tomato sauce, tomato paste, water, and Italian seasoning. Stir well and pour the mixture into the slow cooker.

4. Cover and cook on low for 5 to 6 hours or until the mixture is blended and hot.

5. Cook the spaghetti according to the package directions. Drain and place on serving plates; top with the beef mixture. Sprinkle with Parmesan cheese and serve.

Tamale Pie

Prep time: 15 minutes
Cook time: 6 hours

A tamale pie consists of a meat and bean mixture topped with a corn bread crust. This mixture cooks well in the slow cooker because the corn bread is supposed to stay moist. You can make this recipe spicy or mild, according to your own taste.

½ POUND GROUND PORK

½ CUP CHOPPED ONION

1 GARLIC CLOVE, MINCED

½ JALAPEÑO PEPPER, MINCED

1 TEASPOON CHILI POWDER

½ TEASPOON GROUND CUMIN

ONE 15-OUNCE CAN BLACK BEANS, RINSED AND DRAINED

1 CUP FROZEN CORN KERNELS, THAWED AND DRAINED

ONE 8-OUNCE CAN TOMATO SAUCE

½ CUP SALSA

½ CUP CORNMEAL

½ CUP ALL-PURPOSE FLOUR

¼ TEASPOON BAKING SODA

¼ TEASPOON SALT

3 TABLESPOONS CORN OIL

¼ CUP BUTTERMILK

2 TABLESPOONS SOUR CREAM

1 EGG

1. In a small skillet over medium heat, cook the pork with the onion, garlic, and jalapeño, stirring to break up the meat, until the pork is no longer pink, about 5 minutes. Drain well. Add the chili powder, cumin, black beans, corn, tomato sauce, and salsa to the pan and stir well to combine. Remove the pan from the heat.

2. Pour the pork mixture into the slow cooker.

3. In a small bowl, combine the cornmeal, flour, baking soda, and salt. Add the corn oil, buttermilk, sour cream, and egg; mix just until combined. Spoon the batter over the pork mixture in the slow cooker.

4. Cover and cook on low for 5 to 6 hours or until a toothpick inserted into the corn bread crust comes out clean. Cut the pie into wedges and serve immediately.

Turkey with Stuffing

Prep time: 15 minutes
Cook time: 8 hours

If it's just the two of you, you can get the taste of a real Thanksgiving dinner out of one slow cooker! There will be leftovers, because half of a turkey breast is still a substantial cut of meat. A thick turkey sandwich the day after Thanksgiving is a wonderful treat. Ask the butcher to cut you a half turkey breast, or buy a whole one, cut it in half, and freeze the rest.

1½ CUPS CUBED OATMEAL BREAD
1½ CUPS CUBED WHOLE-WHEAT BREAD
½ CUP CHOPPED ONION
1 GARLIC CLOVE, MINCED
1 CELERY STALK, CHOPPED
½ TEASPOON POULTRY SEASONING
½ TEASPOON DRIED MARJORAM
¼ TEASPOON DRIED SAGE
½ TEASPOON SALT, PLUS MORE FOR SEASONING
FRESHLY GROUND BLACK PEPPER
⅓ CUP LOW SODIUM CHICKEN BROTH
1½- TO 2-POUND BONELESS, SKINLESS TURKEY BREAST HALF
2 TABLESPOONS UNSALTED BUTTER, MELTED

1. Place the bread cubes in a medium bowl. Add the onion, garlic, and celery and toss to combine. Sprinkle in the poultry seasoning, marjoram, sage, salt, and black pepper. Drizzle the broth over the mixture, tossing to coat.

2. Place the stuffing mixture in the slow cooker. Top with the turkey breast. Sprinkle it with more salt and pepper, and drizzle with the butter.

3. Cover and cook on low for 7 to 8 hours, or until the turkey registers 165°F on an instant-read thermometer. Remove the turkey from the slow cooker, tent it with foil, and let it stand for 5 minutes before slicing. Serve with the stuffing.

Cassoulet

Prep time: 15 minutes
Cook time: 7 hours

Cassoulet *is the French word for "casserole." It's traditionally made of beans, vegetables, and several meats including goose, duck confit, and pork sausage. This lighter version is just as delicious and much easier to make. All you need for dinner with this dish is a green salad with a red wine vinegar dressing, some crusty bread, and white wine.*

2 SLICES BACON

½ POUND SMOKED SAUSAGE, SLICED

½ CUP CHOPPED ONION

1 GARLIC CLOVE, MINCED

ONE 14-OUNCE CAN DICED TOMATOES, UNDRAINED

2 TABLESPOONS TOMATO PASTE

¼ CUP DRY RED WINE OR LOW-SODIUM CHICKEN BROTH

½ TEASPOON DRIED THYME

½ TEASPOON DRIED OREGANO

½ TEASPOON SALT

⅛ TEASPOON FRESHLY GROUND BLACK PEPPER

4 BONELESS, SKINLESS CHICKEN THIGHS, CUT INTO 1-INCH CUBES

ONE 15-OUNCE CAN GREAT NORTHERN BEANS, DRAINED AND RINSED

1. In a small skillet over medium heat, cook the bacon until crisp. Remove the bacon from the skillet and drain it on paper towels; crumble and set aside. Drain the fat from the skillet, but do not wipe it out.

2. Add the sliced sausage to the skillet. Cook over medium heat until it is browned on both sides, about 5 minutes total. Remove the sausage from the skillet and place it in the slow cooker.

3. Add the onion and garlic to the skillet. Cook over medium heat, stirring constantly for 3 to 4 minutes to soak up the pan drippings. Add the tomatoes, tomato paste, wine, thyme, oregano, salt, and pepper and bring to a simmer.

4. Add the mixture to the sausage in the slow cooker, along with the bacon. Top with the chicken and beans.

5. Cover and cook on low for 6 to 7 hours or until the chicken is cooked through.

CHAPTER ELEVEN

Desserts

Desserts cooked in the slow cooker are something special. Rich puddings, cheesecake, fruit desserts, and sauces are natural applications, and if you haven't done much baking before, the slow cooker is a great place to start. Just toss in all the ingredients, and come back after dinner when you're ready for something sweet.

However, as easy as these recipes are to make, it's important to note that baked goods are not very tolerant of substitutions. You can't, for instance, add another egg to a slow cooker cake, stir in more flour, and expect good results. Follow the recipe proportions and directions carefully.

These recipes are almost all served warm, except for the cheesecake and rice pudding, and you know that warm desserts are just begging for delicious toppings. Ice cream, whipped cream, and chocolate or caramel sauce are all excellent finishing touches for these creamy and sweet recipes, but feel free to experiment with different textures, too. Slow Cooker Pumpkin Pie is topped with sugar cookies to mimic a crust; Caramel Apple Cake is topped with candied walnuts for some delicious crunch; and velvety Chocolate Fondue is best served with crisp cookies, doughnut holes, and fruit for dipping.

Enjoy these wonderful recipes as the perfect end to your meal.

Chocolate–Peanut Butter Rice Pudding

SERVES 2 TO 3

Prep time: 15 minutes
Cook time: 7½ hours

The amount of rice used in this recipe seems ridiculously low. But the rice is cooked twice, so it really expands. The peanut butter makes the chocolate taste richer and adds more body. You can use almond butter or another nut butter if you like.

½ CUP LONG-GRAIN WHITE RICE
1½ CUPS WATER
1½ CUPS WHOLE MILK
½ CUP SUGAR
¼ CUP HEAVY CREAM
½ TEASPOON PURE VANILLA EXTRACT
½ CUP SEMISWEET CHOCOLATE CHIPS
2 TABLESPOONS PEANUT BUTTER

1. Combine the rice, water, 1 cup of milk, and the sugar in the slow cooker. Cover and cook on low for 5 to 6 hours or until the rice is tender.

2. Stir in the remaining ½ cup of milk along with the cream and vanilla, and cook for 1 more hour.

3. Add the chocolate chips and peanut butter and stir. Cover and cook on low for 20 to 30 minutes longer or until the chocolate melts. Stir again. Serve warm or cold.

Cinnamon Raisin Bread Pudding

SERVES 2

Prep time: 15 minutes

Cook time: 4 hours

Bread pudding is the ultimate sweet comfort food. You can use any type of bread and spices in this easy recipe. It's delicious served with hard sauce: Combine 3 tablespoons of softened butter with 3 tablespoons of sugar and a dash of vanilla extract, and mix until creamy. That's it! You could add a bit of brandy or rum to the hard sauce if you'd like.

3½ CUPS CUBED CINNAMON RAISIN BREAD

1 CUP WHOLE MILK

2 EGGS

2 TABLESPOONS UNSALTED BUTTER, MELTED

3 TABLESPOONS SUGAR

1 TEASPOON PURE VANILLA EXTRACT

¼ TEASPOON GROUND CINNAMON

1. Place the bread in the slow cooker.

2. In a small bowl, whisk together the remaining ingredients. Pour the mixture over the bread in the slow cooker. Let stand for 5 minutes until the bread absorbs the liquid.

3. Cover and cook on low for 4 hours or until a knife inserted near the center comes out clean. Serve warm with hard sauce (see headnote) or ice cream.

Chocolate Cheesecake

SERVES 2

Prep time: 15 minutes
Cook time: 2 hours

You will need two 1-cup custard cups for this recipe. Make sure they are heatproof. This cheesecake is moist and velvety because it cooks in such a moist environment. It should be chilled before you serve it—if you can wait that long!

COOKING SPRAY
2 TEASPOONS ALL-PURPOSE FLOUR, PLUS MORE FOR DUSTING
ONE 8-OUNCE PACKAGE CREAM CHEESE, AT ROOM TEMPERATURE
1 EGG
3 TABLESPOONS SUGAR
2 TABLESPOONS COCOA POWDER
2 TABLESPOONS CHOCOLATE CHIPS, MELTED
½ TEASPOON PURE VANILLA EXTRACT
PINCH OF SALT
¾ CUP WATER

1. Spray two 1-cup custard cups with cooking spray, and dust them with flour, tapping out any excess.

2. Combine the 2 teaspoons of flour, cream cheese, egg, sugar, cocoa powder, chocolate chips, vanilla, and salt in a food processor. Process until smooth, scraping down the sides of the bowl as necessary. You can also beat these ingredients in a small bowl with a mixer. Divide the mixture evenly between the custard cups.

3. Place the cups in the slow cooker. Pour the water around the cups, being careful not to splash any water into them.

4. Cover and cook on high for 2 hours or until the cheesecakes are set. Uncover the slow cooker, turn it off, and let the cheesecakes stand for 30 minutes. Then carefully transfer them to a wire rack; let them cool for another 30 minutes.

5. Cover and refrigerate the cheesecakes for another 3 to 4 hours before serving.

Chocolate Fondue

Prep time: 15 minutes
Cook time: 50 minutes

This fun recipe is so easy to make. Fondue is basically a ganache, which is chocolate melted in cream. For dippers, use doughnut holes, strawberries, small crisp cookies, and grapes. Use a pot holder to remove the cup from the slow cooker, since it will be hot.

1 CUP SEMISWEET CHOCOLATE CHIPS

½ OUNCE UNSWEETENED CHOCOLATE, CHOPPED

½ CUP MILK CHOCOLATE CHIPS

¼ CUP HEAVY CREAM

½ TEASPOON PURE VANILLA EXTRACT

¼ CUP WATER

1. Combine all the chocolate, cream, and vanilla in a 2-cup heatproof custard cup. Place the custard cup in the slow cooker. Pour the water around the custard cup, being careful not to splash any water into it.

2. Cover and cook on low for 40 to 50 minutes or until the chocolate is melted. Stir well, remove the cup from the slow cooker, and serve with dippers.

White Chocolate Sauce with Frozen Fruit

Prep time: 5 minutes
Cook time: 35 minutes

This technique of serving melted chocolate over frozen berries appeared a few years ago in a London restaurant. The hot mixture partially softens the berries, and the berries make the chocolate mixture thicker. It's really sublime. Use a 2-cup slow cooker to make this easy recipe, or put the chocolate mixture into a 2-cup custard cup in a 1½- or 2-quart slow cooker and pour ½ cup water around the cup.

⅔ CUP WHITE CHOCOLATE CHIPS

1 CUP HEAVY CREAM

1 TEASPOON PURE VANILLA EXTRACT

½ TEASPOON FRESHLY GRATED LEMON ZEST

1 CUP FROZEN RASPBERRIES

1 CUP FROZEN BLUEBERRIES

½ CUP FROZEN STRAWBERRIES

½ CUP FROZEN PEACHES, CHOPPED

1. Combine the chocolate chips and cream in the slow cooker.

2. Cover and cook on low for 30 to 35 minutes or until the chocolate is melted. Stir until smooth, then mix in the vanilla and lemon zest.

3. Place the fruit in two serving dishes. Pour the hot sauce over the fruit and serve immediately.

Peach Crumble

Prep time: 15 minutes
Cook time: 2 hours

Crumbles, crisps, and cobblers are all old-fashioned delicious desserts. Crumbles and crisps are made by cooking a sweetened streusel on fruit. Cobblers are made by pouring a batter over fruit and baking. You can use apples in this dessert, but it will need to cook for about double the time.

There are two basic types of peaches: freestone and cling. Both words refer to the peach pit. Freestone peaches come away easily from the pit. With cling peaches, the flesh literally clings to the pit and is difficult to remove. Most cling peaches are sold to canners. But if you have a choice at the supermarket, choose freestone peaches for easy preparation.

5 MEDIUM PEACHES, PEELED AND SLICED 1 INCH THICK
⅓ CUP DRIED CHERRIES
3 TABLESPOONS GRANULATED SUGAR
1 TABLESPOON FRESHLY SQUEEZED LEMON JUICE
2 TEASPOONS CORNSTARCH
PINCH OF SALT
⅛ TEASPOON GROUND NUTMEG
½ CUP ALL-PURPOSE FLOUR
½ CUP ROLLED OATS
1¼ PACKED BROWN SUGAR
½ TEASPOON GROUND CINNAMON
3 TABLESPOONS UNSALTED BUTTER, MELTED
½ CUP CHOPPED PECANS
ICE CREAM, FOR TOPPING (OPTIONAL)

continued ▶

1. Combine the peaches, cherries, granulated sugar, lemon juice, cornstarch, salt, and nutmeg in the slow cooker and toss to coat.

2. In a small bowl, combine the flour, oats, brown sugar, and cinnamon and mix. Add the melted butter and stir until crumbly. Add the pecans, and sprinkle the topping over the fruit in the slow cooker.

3. Cover and cook on high for 1½ to 2 hours or until the peaches are tender and the crumble is bubbling around the edges. Serve with ice cream (if using).

Stuffed Apples

SERVES 2

Prep time: 15 minutes
Cook time: 7 hours

Apples are stuffed with a mixture of nuts and dried fruit and cooked until tender in this homey, old-fashioned recipe. Serve with ice cream or sweetened, softly whipped cream. You can use any type of nut you'd like in this easy dessert, but use an apple variety that's good for cooking, such as Fuji, Granny Smith, or McIntosh.

2 OR 3 APPLES, CORED
3 TABLESPOONS PACKED BROWN SUGAR
2 TABLESPOONS GOLDEN RAISINS
1 TABLESPOON CHOPPED PECANS
¼ TEASPOON GROUND CINNAMON
1 TABLESPOON UNSALTED BUTTER
½ CUP WATER

1. Remove some of the peel from the top of the apples so the skin doesn't split while the apples are cooking.

2. In a small bowl, combine the brown sugar, raisins, pecans, and cinnamon and mix well. Stuff the apples with this mixture and dot with the butter.

3. Place the apples in the slow cooker and pour the water around the apples.

4. Cover and cook on low for 5 to 7 hours or until the apples are tender when pierced with a knife. Let the apples cool slightly before serving.

Turtle Brownies

MAKES 4 BROWNIES

Prep time: 15 minutes
Cook time: 2 hours

Brownies are so moist and dense when cooked in a slow cooker, and the caramel and pecans put this dessert over the top. This recipe makes four brownies, because, really, when is the last time you could eat only one of these fudgy treats? Serve these brownies warm right out of the slow cooker.

COOKING SPRAY
½ CUP ALL-PURPOSE FLOUR, PLUS MORE FOR DUSTING
2 TABLESPOONS UNSALTED BUTTER, MELTED
1 TABLESPOON VEGETABLE OIL
¼ CUP PACKED BROWN SUGAR
¼ CUP GRANULATED SUGAR
1 EGG, BEATEN
¼ CUP SEMISWEET CHOCOLATE CHIPS, MELTED
1 TEASPOON PURE VANILLA EXTRACT
2 TABLESPOONS COCOA POWDER
¼ CUP CARAMEL SAUCE
2 TABLESPOONS CHOPPED PECANS

1. Line the slow cooker with foil and create a foil sling (see page 8). Spray the foil with cooking spray, and dust with flour, tapping out any excess.

2. In a small bowl, combine the butter and oil. Beat in both of the sugars until combined. Beat in the egg, and then beat in the melted chocolate chips. Add the vanilla.

3. Stir in ½ cup of flour and the cocoa powder until combined.

4. Pour the batter into the slow cooker. Cover and cook on high for 1 hour. Then drizzle the batter with the caramel sauce and sprinkle with the pecans.

5. Cover and cook on high for 40 to 60 minutes longer, until a toothpick inserted in the center comes out almost clean. Remove the brownies from the slow cooker using the foil sling, and let them cool on a wire rack. Cut into wedges to serve.

Caramel Apple Cake

Prep time: 15 minutes
Cook time: 2 hours

This slow cooker recipe yields a very tender and moist cake. Serve it with some warmed caramel sauce and a scoop of butter pecan ice cream for the perfect dessert. You'll need a 5-inch round baking pan to make this dessert.

COOKING SPRAY

1 CUP ALL-PURPOSE FLOUR, PLUS MORE FOR DUSTING

⅛ TEASPOON SALT

½ TEASPOON BAKING POWDER

½ TEASPOON BAKING SODA

⅓ CUP PACKED BROWN SUGAR

5 TABLESPOONS UNSALTED BUTTER, MELTED

1 EGG, BEATEN

1 TABLESPOON WHOLE MILK

½ TEASPOON PURE VANILLA EXTRACT

⅓ CUP PEELED, CORED, AND FINELY CHOPPED APPLE

¼ CUP CARAMEL SAUCE

1. Spray a 5-inch round baking pan with cooking spray and dust it with flour, tapping out any excess. Set aside.

2. In a medium bowl, combine 1 cup of flour with the salt, baking powder, baking soda, and brown sugar and mix well. Stir in the melted butter, egg, milk, and vanilla until combined. Stir in the apple.

3. Pour the caramel sauce into the bottom of the prepared pan. Top with the batter, and place the pan in the slow cooker.

4. Cover and cook on high for 1½ to 2 hours or until the cake springs back when lightly touched with your finger.

5. Remove the pan from the slow cooker and let the cake cool in the pan for 10 minutes, then run a knife around the edge of the pan. Invert the cake onto a serving plate. Serve warm.

Slow Cooker Pumpkin Pie

SERVES 2 TO 3

Prep time: 15 minutes
Cook time: 6 hours

This dense and creamy pumpkin pie is topped with sugar cookies to mimic a crust. The contrast in texture is really delightful. Make sure you use canned pumpkin for this recipe, not pumpkin pie filling, which contains sugar, spices, and other ingredients.

COOKING SPRAY
¼ CUP ALL-PURPOSE FLOUR
1½ CUPS SOLID-PACK PUMPKIN
ONE 5-OUNCE CAN EVAPORATED MILK
3 TABLESPOONS HEAVY CREAM
⅓ CUP PACKED BROWN SUGAR
2 EGGS, BEATEN
2 TABLESPOONS UNSALTED BUTTER, MELTED
½ TEASPOON GROUND CINNAMON
⅛ TEASPOON GROUND NUTMEG
⅛ TEASPOON GROUND CARDAMOM
1 TEASPOON PURE VANILLA EXTRACT
2 TO 3 SUGAR COOKIES, CRUSHED

1. Spray the slow cooker with cooking spray and dust it with 1 tablespoon of the flour, tapping out any excess. Set aside.

2. In a medium bowl, combine the remainder of flour with the pumpkin, evaporated milk, cream, brown sugar, egg, butter, cinnamon, nutmeg, cardamom, and vanilla. Beat until smooth. Pour the mixture into the slow cooker.

3. Cover and cook on low for 4 to 6 hours or until the pie is set and an instant-read thermometer registers 165°F. Scoop the pie filling out of the slow cooker and top with the cookies to serve.

Substitutions and Equivalents

When you're cooking for two, you often use up only part of a can or jar of ingredients. It's helpful to know how much each can holds so you can plan another recipe using the rest of the contents. And when a recipe calls for 1 cup of shredded cheese, for example, do you know how much cheese to buy? This chart will help you make the most of your pantry.

Ingredient	Equivalent
½ pound cheese	2 cups shredded cheese
1 egg	¼ cup egg substitute
14 saltine crackers	½ cup crumbs
6 graham cracker squares	½ cup crumbs
1 slice bread	⅓ cup fresh soft bread crumbs
3 cups cornflakes cereal	1 cup crumbs
12-ounce package chocolate chips	2 cups
1 medium onion	½ cup chopped
10 vanilla wafers	½ cup crumbs
1 cup uncooked pasta	2½ cups cooked
1 cup barley	3½ cups cooked
1 cup wild rice	3 cups cooked
1 cup long-grain white rice	3 cups cooked
1 stick butter	½ cup or 4 ounces
15-ounce container ricotta cheese	2 cups
14-ounce can diced tomatoes	scant 2 cups

Ingredient	Equivalent
15-ounce can beans	1½ cups
8-ounce can tomato sauce	1 cup
6-ounce can tomato paste	12 tablespoons
26-ounce jar spaghetti sauce	3 cups
1 apple	1 cup sliced; ¾ cup chopped
1 lemon	3 tablespoons juice and 1 teaspoon zest
8 ounces nuts	¾ cup chopped

Buying a Slow Cooker

Buying a slow cooker is as easy as buying any other kitchen item. Read about the different brands below to select the one that suits you best. You can buy them online and at many grocery stores and big-box retailers. Always read the instruction booklet that comes with the slow cooker before you start using it.

Crock-Pot

The smallest size this company makes is a 2-quart slow cooker; they also have a $2\frac{1}{2}$-quart size. These slow cookers have settings of low, high, and keep warm, and come with a removable round stoneware insert. Crock-Pot also makes a Little Dipper slow cooker with a 16-ounce, or 2-cup, capacity. The insert is not removable on this appliance. Crock-Pot is also the maker of the buffet cooker, which holds three $1\frac{1}{2}$-quart removable stoneware crocks that are ideal for cooking an entire meal for two. In addition, they make a Hook Up Connectable Entertaining System that can connect up to six units using one outlet. The individual slow cookers come in 1-quart, 2-quart, and $3\frac{1}{2}$-quart capacities and in various configurations.

Hamilton Beach

This company's 3-in-1 slow cooker has 2-quart, 4-quart, and 6-quart inserts. The base is stainless steel, and the removable inserts are made from stoneware. The same glass lid fits all of the inserts.

Maxi-Matic

The $1\frac{1}{2}$-quart slow cooker from Maxi-Matic has a removable stoneware pot and low, high, and keep warm settings. It also boasts a stainless steel finish and cool-touch handles.

Proctor Silex

Proctor Silex makes several $1\frac{1}{2}$-quart slow cookers. One is round with a removable stoneware crock. The settings are low, high, and keep warm. It measures about 8-by-8-by-9 inches. The other is oval, with a removable insert and a lid latch strap so you can travel with the slow cooker. It also has low, high, and keep warm settings.

Rival

This company makes a 2-quart slow cooker with a removable ceramic insert; high, low, and warm settings; and a glass lid.

Recipe Index

Index

CPSIA information can be obtained
at www.ICGtesting.com
Printed in the USA
JSHW061532280323
39591JS00004B/32

9 781623 153861